S0-AKA-087

THOMAS HOBBES

British History in Perspective
General Editor: Jeremy Black

PUBLISHED TITLES

Rodney Barker *Politics, Peoples and Government*
C. J. Bartlett *British Foreign Policy in the Twentieth Century*
Jeremy Black *Robert Walpole and the Nature of Politics in Early Eighteenth-Century Britain*
Anne Curry *The Hundred Years War*
John W. Derry *British Politics in the Age of Fox, Pitt and Liverpool*
William Gibson *Church, State and Society, 1760–1850*
Brian Golding *Conquest and Colonisation: the Normans in Britain, 1066–1100*
S. J. Gunn *Early Tudor Government, 1485–1558*
Richard Harding *The Evolution of the Sailing Navy, 1509–1815*
Ann Hughes *The Causes of the English Civil War*
Ronald Hutton *The British Republic, 1649–1660*
Kevin Jefferys *The Labour Party since 1945*
T. A. Jenkins *Disraeli and Victorian Conservatism*
D. M. Loades *The Mid-Tudor Crisis, 1545–1565*
Diarmaid MacCulloch *The Later Reformation in England, 1547–1603*
A. P. Martinich *Thomas Hobbes*
W. M. Ormrod *Political Life in Medieval England, 1300–1450*
Keith Perry *British Politics and the American Revolution*
A. J. Pollard *The Wars of the Roses*
David Powell *British Politics and the Labour Question, 1868–1990*
David Powell *The Edwardian Crisis*
Richard Rex *Henry VIII and the English Reformation*
G. R. Searle *The Liberal Party: Triumph and Disintegration, 1886–1929*
Paul Seaward *The Restoration, 1660–1668*
W. M. Spellman *John Locke*
Robert Stewart *Party and Politics, 1830–1852*
John W. Young *Britain and European Unity, 1945–92*
Michael B. Young *Charles I*

History of Ireland

D. G. Boyce *The Irish Question and British Politics, 1868–1996 (2nd edn)*
Seán Duffy *Ireland in the Middle Ages*
David Harkness *Ireland in the Twentieth Century: Divided Island*

History of Scotland

Keith M. Brown *Kingdom or Province? Scotland and the Regal Union, 1603–1715*
Bruce Webster *Medieval Scotland*

History of Wales

A. D. Carr *Medieval Wales*
J. Gwynfor Jones *Early Modern Wales, c.1525–1640*

Thomas Hobbes

A. P. Martinich
Department of Philosophy
University of Texas at Austin

St. Martin's Press
New York

For information, address:

St. Martin's Press, Scholarly and Reference Division,
175 Fifth Avenue, New York, N.Y. 10010

First published in the United States of America in 1997

Printed in Hong Kong

ISBN 0–312–16493–9 (cloth)
ISBN 0–312–16494–7 (paperback)

Library of Congress Cataloging-in-Publication Data
Martinich, Aloysius.
Thomas Hobbes / A. P. Martinich.
p. cm. — (British history in perspective)
Includes bibliographical references and index.
ISBN 0–312–16493–9 (cloth). — ISBN 0–312–16494–7 (pbk.)
1. Hobbes, Thomas, 1588–1679. I. Title. II. Series.
B1247.M37 1997
192—dc20 96–28495
[B] CIP

To Leslie, again

CONTENTS

Acknowledgements

I want to thank Jeremy Black, who invited me to contribute this volume. His own scholarship in eighteenth-century English studies matches the highest standards I have claimed for Hobbesian scholarship. Max Rosenkrantz and Kinch Hoekstra gave especially detailed and incisive comments. Others who gave helpful comments on the manuscript in whole or in part include David Johnston, Fred Kronz, Brian Levack, Leslie Martinich and Jon Rosenthal. I am grateful to the anonymous reviewer for his or her comments. I also want to thank Vanessa Graham and Simon Winder, my publishers at Macmillan.

A. P. Martinich

A Note on References

References to *Leviathan* are given with chapter and paragraph number, e.g. *L* 13.1. References to the editions by Molesworth are given by volume and page number, e.g. *EW* 3: 157. References to works that have chapters and section are cited by giving them.

Abbreviations

AW	*Anti-White (Thomas White's De Mundo Examined)*, tr. Harold Jones
B	*Behemoth*, ed. Ferdinand Tonnies
DC	*De Cive*
DCo	*De Corpore*
EL	*Elements of Law, Natural and Politic*
EW	*English Works*, ed. Sir William Molesworth
L	*Leviathan*
OL	*Opera Latina*, ed. Sir Wiliam Molesworth

INTRODUCTION

Hobbes's reputation as a thinker has never been higher. As famous and influential as he was between 1640 and 1700, his importance is even greater today. His uncompromising naturalism, scientism[1] and jaundiced view of human nature agree with the temper of the times. His current popularity in large part explains the great quantity and the high quality of Hobbesian scholarship over the last quarter-century or so. One consequence is that Hobbes has never been so well understood as he is today. I make this claim even though the spectrum of opinion about 'what Hobbes really meant' is astonishingly wide. To some he is an atheist; to a few he is a sincere, if idiosyncratic, Christian. To some he is a democrat; to most he is an absolutist. To some he is an empiricist; to others he is a rationalist. Although these dichotomies may seem to be incompatible, whether they are in actuality depends upon how the terms are defined and what criteria are applied. For example, Bishop Henry Hammond called Hobbes a 'Christian atheist'; taken literally, it is not clear either what that phrase means or what criterion is supposed to apply for its use. In the body of this book, I shall explain the senses in which Hobbes is simultaneously a democrat and an absolutist, an empiricist and a rationalist, a Christian and yet a patron saint of contemporary atheism.

In his own day, Hobbes was not studied as attentively and closely as he is today. His contemporaries, friend and foe alike, obviously did not have the advantage of three centuries to investigate and reflect on his life and work. Even if there is no progress in philosophy, there is progress in the history of philosophy.[2]

A remarkable feature of this scholarship on Hobbes is its interdisciplinary character. It is not simply that he is studied by historians, philosophers, political theorists and historians of science, religion and literature, but that many of these scholars use (and often debate) the work of their cross-discipline colleagues. Everything has its down side. For the marvellous resurgence of interest in Hobbes, it is the impossibility of reading all of the scholarship on Hobbes's thought, much less mastering it. So a prime goal of this book is to acquaint the reader with the best contemporary scholarship on the broad range of Hobbes's thought. My own interpretation is intended to capture most closely what Hobbes himself believed in the context of the seventeenth century and to explain those views more clearly than he did himself. It is not my intention to improve upon his views. (I will, however, be reporting the work of some scholars who do try to improve on him.)

When alternative interpretations of his views are presented, they are intended either to advance the understanding of what he actually did hold or to acquaint the reader with important alternative readings.

Much of the spelling and punctuation of seventeenth-century texts has been modernized; and 'then' has often been changed to 'than' for the sake of clarity.

1

THE LIFE OF THOMAS HOBBES

Childhood

Thomas Hobbes was at Magdalen Hall, Oxford, when James VI of Scotland in 1603 initiated the Stuart monarchy in England as James I.[1] Hobbes died in 1679, just as the the Popish Plot was beginning to thicken. Therefore, virtually all of his intellectual life coincided with the early and middle Stuart period. He was involved in one way or another with the controversies over Ship Money, Forced Loans, the foundations of the sovereignty of James I and Charles I, the nature and function of their parliaments, the English Civil War, the legitimacy of the Commonwealth, the nature and practice of scientists such as Robert Boyle and William Harvey and mathematicians such as John Wallis. To study Hobbes's life is to gain a perspective on a large part of Stuart England. Because of his peculiar genius, it is an unconventional one. Although he was on the Continent several times for a total of twenty years, profited greatly from those excursions, and was probably more revered there than in his native land, he was always an Englishman at heart.[2] Many of the people he associated with on the Continent were fellow exiles. After being in self-imposed exile from 1640 until 1651, he returned to England after the fighting of the English Civil War had ended and some stability had been achieved. He preferred to live under an English government that abhorred his professed doctrine of absolute sovereignty than under a French one that practised it. Even when he was persecuted by the royalist churchmen during the Restoration, he stayed and defended himself rather than taking refuge in a religiously more tolerant land such as the Netherlands.

Hobbes was born on 5 April 1588, in Westport, a village then on the outskirts of Malmesbury.[3] Although the Spanish Armada did not set sail until May, the impending invasion was rumoured all through the year. There was no way for Wiltshire people to be sure of when the fleet would set sail, where it would invade, and how many troops might be landed to move inland and take over the entire country. As Hobbes would point out decades later, when one does not know at what particular time an enemy will attack, one must always be on guard against it. So it is plausible that it is literally true, as he reported, that his birth was premature and induced by his mother's fear of the Spanish Armada. Of course, his further report that that his mother gave birth at the same time to a twin – namely, Fear – is only figuratively true.

Hobbes's father, Thomas senior, was a minister of the Church of England, but not an exemplary one. On one occasion, he fell asleep during the worship service and was heard to mutter that clubs were trumps. Some time later he scuffled with another minister in front of the church, and fled Westport and its environs for the rest of his life. He reportedly settled near London; but there is no evidence that Hobbes ever saw him again. Fortunately, Hobbes's paternal uncle, a well-to-do glove-maker, looked after the family financially and educationally. Hobbes started his schooling at the age of four. His favourite teacher was Robert Latimer, whose *alma mater,* Magdalen Hall, Oxford, Hobbes chose to attend.

With the Cavendishes

Hobbes was not an assiduous student at Oxford. By his own account, he did not like the curriculum. He enjoyed capturing jackdaws and spent a large part of his time visiting map shops, where he marvelled over the discovery of the new lands of America and daydreamed about the parts labelled 'terra incognita'. Decades later, his friend, the poet Abraham Cowley, would refer to him as a Columbus of science. Hobbes graduated in February 1608 and 'determined' (that is, passed certain oral examinations) the following Lent.

Hobbes must have had some obvious intellectual and social talents, because the principal recommended him to the wealthy William Cavendish to tutor his son, also named William. Since there was only a three-year difference between them, Hobbes was as much a companion to the young William as he was a tutor. Young William was fun-loving to a fault. On the Devonshire estates, he and Hobbes spent a lot of time hawking and riding together. In London, William probably engaged in all of the normal activities of an unemployed son of a rich aristocrat, with Hobbes in tow. William's tastes were expensive, and it would have been both embarrassing and time-consuming if he had gone out in search of loans to finance his lifestyle. So Hobbes did it for him. In general, Hobbes had a winning personality and was well-liked by the family.[4] At the death of his father in 1626, William became the second Earl of Devonshire.

Hobbes's association with the Cavendish family was one of the happiest accidents of seventeenth-century politics, philosophy and science. There were two main branches of that family; and it was the other branch, namely, that headed by the person who would eventually become the Duke of Newcastle, that was much more important. Newcastle – he too a William Cavendish – became an important political player and a patron of the scientific circle of England and France. Finally, Newcastle's younger brother Charles was a competent mathematician and an admirer of Hobbes.

A standard part of a young gentleman's education was to tour the Continent. Therefore, the young William set off with Hobbes at some time after 1610 to broaden their horizons. In Venice, William met Fulgenzio Micanzio, a friend of Paolo Sarpi, who was assisting his government in opposing the Pope's attempted domination of Venice. Sarpi, who published a number of works, most notably a history of the Council of Trent that criticized papal pretensions to supremacy, was interested in England's papal problems because they paralleled those of Venice. William corresponded with Micanzio after he returned to England in 1615. Hobbes translated these letters from Italian into English. Hobbes and William also spent time in Rome. During this first tour, Hobbes discovered that the scholastic philosophy and logic that he had been taught at Oxford was in disrepute among the bright young intellectuals of Europe. He was happy to hear of it and concentrated his instruction to William on French and Italian.

After his return to England in 1615,[5] Hobbes devoted a substantial amount of time to reading romances and plays.[6] He also studied ancient historians and poets at about this time. His favourite was Thucydides, whose *History of the Peloponnesian Wars* he would eventually translate.

At some time between 1618 and 1622, Hobbes seems to have served as a secretary to Francis Bacon, who thought that Hobbes was one of the few people to understand his philosophy. With regard to the philosophy of science, Bacon was a radical empiricist and Hobbes a radical rationalist. Bacon thought that after a wholesale collection of observable facts, science would emerge by putting them into order. Hobbes thought that science was strictly deductive and that it needed to begin with definitions (see Chapter 4). Therefore, they are at opposite ends of the spectrum of opinions about proper scientific method. However, they agreed about the bankruptcy of Aristotelianism, the need for clarity and precision, and the idea that the point of having knowledge is power or control. It is to Hobbes that we owe the story about Bacon's death, the result of stopping to stuff a dead chicken with snow in order to test the preservative power of cold.

From 1622 until it was dissolved in 1624, Hobbes was a member of the Virginia Company. William had given him one share as part of a scheme to increase the voting strength of one faction of shareholders. In view of Hobbes's participation in the company, it may seem odd that Hobbes would exhibit such a naïve view of America in his later writings; but it is plausible that the information given to the members of the Virginia Company was similarly naïve.

The mid-1620s were filled with political unrest. Charles I had succeeded his father in 1625, and the honeymoon between the king and Parliament was short-lived. There was both a theoretical and a practical struggle between them. The practical struggle concerned Charles's desire to run the country without the interference of Parliament. Unfortunately for him, Parliament controlled the major sources of taxation available. Desperate for money in 1626–7, Charles forced his subjects to lend him money. As the secretary to the earl, Hobbes helped to collect this money in Derbyshire.

The theoretical struggle concerned Charles's desire, like his father's, to be recognized as an absolute sovereign. Hobbes sided with Charles and supported the king's case in a rather oblique way. He translated Thucydides' *History of the Peloponnesian Wars* in order to warn his fellow Englishmen of the dangers of listening to the rhetoric of people other than those who supported the sovereign. Hobbes presumably intended people to read his translation and to see the similarities between the self-destructiveness of the Greek city–states and England. The translation was first published in 1629.[7] His former tutee, William Cavendish, had died the year before, having expired from too much good living. Hobbes was very fond of him and dedicated his translation to his late master in the form of a letter addressed to the son, William, the third Earl of Devonshire.

Hobbes's own health seems to have improved at about this time. Aubrey reports that Hobbes had been sickly as a youth with a yellowish complexion; but he acquired a 'fresh, ruddy, complexion' after the age of forty.[8] Aubrey says that Hobbes was '*sanguineo-melancholicus*, which the physiologers say is the most ingenious complexion'. When he laughed, his hazel eyes became slits, and his pupils could hardly be seen. When he was serious, his eyes opened widely. He was above average in height, about six feet tall.[9] In youth, his black hair had earned him the nickname 'Crow'. As he aged, it turned from reddish white to white. He kept his hair at shoulder length even when the top of his head became bald in the characteristic male pattern. He had a full moustache but only a tuft of whiskers beneath his lower lip. His skin was smooth, with large pores. His moustache and small beard were 'yellowish–reddish'.[10]

Before his death, the second earl had succeeded in jeopardizing the finances of his branch of the family. His wife Christian devised an aggressive strategy to solve her economic problems. Hobbes was let go, but whether it was for financial reasons or because she partially blamed him for her late husband's profligacy is unknown. It was not difficult for Hobbes to find another position. Sir Gervase Clifton, a neighbour of the Newcastle branch of the Cavendishes, employed Hobbes, now forty, as a tutor to his son. As in the first case, Hobbes accompanied the son to the Continent. It was during this time, in about 1630, that Hobbes became enamoured with geometry. Waiting in some gentleman's study, he happened to read the Pythagorean theorem and its proof in Euclid's *Geometry*: 'By God, this is impossible,' he exclaimed; but he read the proof of the previous theorem because it had been used in the last. This proof led him further back to others. At the beginning of the book were axioms and postulates. Hobbes was smitten by the power and the orderliness of a deductive system. Geometry would eventually become his paradigm of science.[11]

After the tour with young Gervase ended in 1630, Hobbes returned to the employment of the Devonshire Cavendishes. Formally, he resumed his job as tutor to the third Earl of Devonshire, still another William Cavendish. In fact, there was plenty of time for his own private study and for interaction with the scientific circle around the Newcastle Cavendishes who met at Welbeck Abbey, the group of intellectuals that gravitated to Lucius Cary's residence at Great Tew, and later to Marin Mersenne's circle in France. The chief investigators at Welbeck Abbey were Charles Cavendish, Robert Payne, John Pell and Walter Warner. The leading lights at Great Tew were William Chillingworth, Dudley Digges, John Hales, Edward Hyde and Jeremy Taylor. There were various relationships of blood, marriage and friendship that connected the two groups. The principal interests of the Welbeck group were science and mathematics; those of the Great Tew group were religion and its relation to politics. By 1634, Hobbes had acquired a reputation as a formidable theorist about optics. His reputation in politics and religion would not come for another decade.

It was also in the year 1634 that Hobbes made his next trip to Europe, now as tutor to the third Earl of Devonshire. He met Galileo, who was imprisoned by the Inquisition but still relatively free to receive visitors. Galileo was impressive; he was one of the few people whom Hobbes credits as advancing science. Hobbes adopted one of Galileo's basic ideas, namely, the principle of inertia: a thing in motion remains in motion unless acted upon in a contrary way; and a thing at rest remains at rest until something moves it.

Hobbes also became a member of Marin Mersenne's scientific circle. From this group, Pierre Gassendi became one of Hobbes's closest friends, and René Descartes became one of his worst enemies. All three tried to give materialistic explanations for the world of motion. They differed in that Gassendi and Descartes nonetheless thought that there were immaterial souls, while Hobbes was an uncompromising materialist. On the Continent, Hobbes continued his work on optics; but he also read and theorized about the nature of sovereignty, on issues concerning religion and even the movements of horses. In addition, Hobbes had a plan for a philosophical psychology, that is, an explanation of the 'faculties and passions of the soul'.

Shortly after Hobbes returned to England in October 1637, he was sent a copy of Descartes's *Discourse on the Method of Rightly Conducting the Reason.* One of the several appendices to the *Discourse* was a theory of vision, according to which, colour is not a part of a material object but is caused by that object acting on the perceiver's optical nerves. In the 1640s, Hobbes insisted that he had been the first to have thought of this, in 1630.

Although there are manuscripts dating from the late 1630s and the mid-1640s on Hobbes's scientific views,[12] these would not be sufficiently polished or complete enough to warrant publication until 1655 at the earliest. First would come his political work.

Charles's relations with the greater part of politically engaged England continued to deteriorate during the 1630s. No Parliament met during that decade. In 1639, he perpetrated a war with Scotland and was easily defeated. He made an insincere treaty in order to buy time. On 13 April 1640, the first Parliament in eleven years opened. Charles's intention was to persuade it to approve money for him to conduct another war against Scotland. Parliament had a different agenda and in any case did not see the point of fighting Protestant Scotland, especially when they feared that Catholic Ireland was a greater threat. Thus, Charles dissolved the Short Parliament of 1640 on 5 May.

Hobbes's dedication of *The Elements of Law, Natural and Politic* was dated 9 May. (Years later, Hobbes would remember the work as circulating during the Short Parliament.) The political parts of *The Elements of Law* are a theoretical defence of absolute sovereignty, with a strong preference asserted for monarchy. A number of influential parliamentarians were very unhappy about this work. (Quite a few copies seemed to be in circulation. The British Library itself has several copies in various states of completeness.) It was a secular version of the position that Roger Manwaring and Robert Sibthorp had taken in the late 1620s. Soon after the Long Parliament opened, Archbishop William Laud and the Earl of Strafford were imprisoned and eventually executed. Speeches were given against those who had inflamed the divisions between the king and Parliament.

Exile

Fearing for his own safety, Hobbes left for the Continent in November, just after the Long Parliament opened. He would not return until the winter of 1651–2. By that time a slightly altered version of *The Elements of Law* had been published in two parts without Hobbes's supervision. The first was titled *Humane Nature* and the second *De Corpore Politico*. When Hobbes arrived on the Continent in 1640, he continued his political reflections. He dedicated *De Cive* to the Earl of Devonshire on 1 November 1641. It was published in a small print run, probably at the suggestion of Mersenne, in April 1642. Its complete title, *Elementorum Philosophiae Sectio Tertia De Cive*, indicated that it was the third part of a trilogy that would be a comprehensive treatment of philosophy. The first two parts, *De Corpore* (1655) and *De Homine* (1658), were probably worked out in Hobbes's head but not set down in final form for many years. A second expanded edition of *De Cive* was published by the Dutch publishing company Elzevir in 1647.

Hobbes flourished in the company of Mersenne and his circle. He authored one of the six sets of objections to Descartes's *Meditations*. But Hobbes and Descartes were mutually unimpressed. Hobbes was an uncompromising materialist and monist, while Descartes was an uncompromising dualist. Hobbes thought that Descartes was a 'good geometrician' and that he should have restricted his study to mathematics. Descartes thought that Hobbes had no talent for metaphysics. If he had only lived to read Hobbes's numerous attempts to square the circle, one can imagine what he would have said about Hobbes's talent as a mathematician. Hobbes was better at exploring the foundations of mathematics and science than at expanding its frontiers. He believed that certainty had to be grounded in the definitions that formed the axioms of science, while Descartes thought that certainty had to be grounded in the 'cogito', that is, the experience of one's own existence in the process of thinking.

A large part of their mutual dislike was due to their similarity. Each jealously promoted his own originality and reputation and – aside from Descartes's mentalism – they were remarkably similar in their philosophies. Both aspired to give completely mechanistic explanations for all physical reality. Both thought deeply about the nature of light and optics; and both wanted to apply mathematics to physics. Although each failed to devise a cogent scientific theory, the spirit of their projects, namely, to develop a mechanistic explanation for physical reality, is more significant than the degree of their success.[13]

In addition to the Frenchmen, Hobbes had many English exiles to associate with. Between 1642 and 1643, Hobbes wrote a critique of Thomas White's *De Mundo*; many of Hobbes's own ideas expressed in this manuscript would be worked out in *De Corpore.* As the king's side in the Civil War deteriorated, more royalists came to France, notably the then Marquis of Newcastle, who had left England after the defeat at Marston Moor. In 1645, Hobbes debated with John Bramhall in front of the marquis. Each then wrote down his views, with the understanding that the material would not be published. In 1654, Hobbes's contribution was published without his knowledge, as *Of Liberty and Necessity.* Bramhall, feeling betrayed, responded with his own manuscript. Hobbes then answered in 1656 with *The Questions Concerning Liberty, Necessity, and Chance,* which contains the complete text of the preceding works mentioned, plus Hobbes's response to Bramhall. In 1657, Bramhall had the last word on this subject by publishing *Castigations of Hobbes's Animadversions.*

In 1646, Hobbes planned to go to stay with friends in the district of Languedoc, so that he could complete *The Elements of Philosophy.* But when he was invited to tutor the exiled Prince of Wales, the future Charles II, in mathematics, he decided to stay in Paris. Although it is usually believed that he gained his position through the efforts of Newcastle, there is strong evidence that the appointment came through the recommendation of Henry Jermyn, who later described Hobbes as 'the oddest fellow' he ever met. Samuel Sorbiere, who arranged the 1647 edition of *De Cive,* had a portrait of Hobbes placed at the front of the volume with the inscription, 'Nobilis Anglus Ser[enissimo] Principi Walliae a studiis praepositus' ('An honoured Englishman, governor of studies to the most serene Prince of Wales'). Hobbes took exception to the title. For one thing, he was not a member of the royal household; and the prince's reputation might be sullied by being associated with Hobbes. For another, he may have wanted not to be tied too closely to the exiled court. As much as he may have liked the company he kept in France, his heart was in England, and he wanted to return. Also, the clergy around the royal court in exile had turned against him and, even though he had many Roman Catholic friends, the French clergy were unhappy with his anti-Catholic views (*OL* 1:xvii).

Notwithstanding his teaching duties, Hobbes had time to work on his philosophy. But the work went slowly, and in mid-August 1647, he became seriously ill for about six weeks. Mersenne tried to convert him to Roman Catholicism, but Hobbes remained firmly committed to the Church of England. He gratefully received the eucharist from an Anglican churchman, John Cosin, and confessed to another Anglican, John Pierson.[14]

As the third part of his comprehensive and scientific treatment of philosophy, *De Cive* did not stand alone and was supposedly a strictly deductive treatise, too austere for most readers. What was needed was a fuller, more accessible treatment of the relevant topics, something that discussed human nature in addition to political philosophy, and something that talked about proper and improper relationships between Christianity and commonwealths. Finally, it needed to be written in an engaging, persuasive way. The result was *Leviathan* which, although written in France, was published in England in May 1651. A powerful case has been made that while in *De Cive* Hobbes emphasized the place of political theory within his general scheme of philosophy, in *Leviathan* he wanted to integrate 'theological and metaphysical argumentation' into his political views. According to one influential interpretation, Hobbes wanted to change his culture, not merely provide the foundations for political theory.[15]

Return of the Native

Hobbes arrived back in England in the winter of 1651–2; he was sixty-three and beginning to show his age. While still in

France, Hobbes developed a 'shaking palsy in his hands'. It worsened, and his handwriting eventually became illegible. He employed various amanuenses to write his manuscripts. His favourite was James Weldon, the Earl of Devonshire's baker. Weldon became something of a butler to Hobbes in his later years and was appointed by him as the executor of his will.[16]

Sentiment aside, there were several reasons for returning to England. He had been excluded from the royal court, due either to the animosity of the English clergy or that of English Roman Catholics; royalists had assassinated two of their enemies, Anthony Ascham and Isaac Dorislaus, in European countries; and the French clergy were unhappy with his anti-Catholicism.

In 1650, the Commonwealth government had begun to require that all adult males take an Engagement Oath, which declared their loyalty to the new government. Since his view was that a person could give consent to be governed by any entity that had sufficient power to protect him, Hobbes did not have any moral problem with taking the oath. Other Englishmen were not in such a morally comfortable position. Those who had taken the Solemn League and Covenant in 1643 had sworn to defend the king. The leaders of the Commonwealth government had been responsible for both the execution of Charles I and the abolition of the monarchy, so men of integrity seemed to be barred from taking the oath; yet the government seemed to be legitimate in the sense that it was the only entity in England serving the functions of a government. This problematic state of affairs led to the publication of a series of pamphlets, devoted to the so-called Engagement Controversy. The doctrine of *Leviathan* supported the position that the Commonwealth was legitimate. In a pre-Restoration work, Hobbes even bragged that his work had persuaded 'a thousand gentlemen' to obey the government.[17]

One of the notorious theories of that controversy was the so-called *de facto* theory, according to which any *de facto* government is by that very fact legitimate, even if unlawful, according to some accepted law. While Hobbes's theory can be used to show how people on the losing side can in good conscience pledge allegiance to the winning side, he is not a *de facto* theorist. For Hobbes, a government, in addition to having the power to enforce its will, must have the consent of the people.[18]

Leviathan was a multi-faceted work, and it could be used to support all sorts of positions. At the Restoration, Hobbes could rightly point out that 'there is scarce a page' that does not attack the enemies of Charles I (*EW* 4:414). Ostensibly, *Leviathan* also defended a theory of the proper relation between a Christian church and state, very close to that of James I. The theory was undoubtedly Erastian, but Erastianism had been the official view of England since the sixteenth century, and a majority of the members of the Long Parliament were probably Erastian.[19] *Leviathan* was also considered atheistic. A committee of Parliament considered a complaint of atheism against *Leviathan* in 1657, but no action was taken. Other complaints to Parliament would be considered during the Restoration, again with no resulting sanctions.

Although many people hated Hobbes because of *Leviathan*, it solidified his reputation as a philosopher. It was also his last substantive work in political philosophy. A Latin translation appeared in Holland in 1668, with some interesting variations from the English version, but they do not significantly add to or change the doctrine that he had worked out between 1640 and 1651. After 1651, Hobbes devoted most of his intellectual efforts to mathematics, science and religion. Concerning science, he still needed to complete the trilogy that he had hoped to publish in the 1640s. In 1655, the first part, *De Corpore,* was published, followed in 1658 by *De Homine. De Corpore* is a competent and interesting work, containing Hobbes's views about language, logic, philosophical and scientific method, physics and geometry. An English translation, containing some revised chapters, appeared the next year. The identity of the translator is debated. While some hold that Hobbes did it himself, and indeed he must have done some of it, the weight of scholarly opinion is moving in the direction of maintaining that some unidentified person other than Hobbes did most of it. *De Homine* is a disappointment and was probably published for the most part simply to wrap up the trilogy. About half of it is a treatise on optics, very similar in content to a longer manuscript, *A Minute or First Draught of the Optiques*, written in 1646. Nonetheless, the trilogy *The Elements of Philosophy* is important as an early version of the unity of science. While he realized that political theory was the science that he had presented most cogently, he thought that he had 'demonstrated the nature of the senses ... the principles of optics, natural light, the cause of reflection and refraction ... [and] the derivation of gravity'.[20]

Hobbes, always a royalist sympathizer even when he lived under the Commonwealth and Protectorate, must have rejoiced at the Restoration. However, he still had enemies at court, mostly restored Laudian clergymen who supported the king but not his doctrine of absolute sovereignty. It was easy for his enemies to make complaints against him. He had returned to England when his king was still in exile; he had taken the Engagement Oath; and *Leviathan* had been used by proponents of reconciliation with the Commonwealth. He opposed the doctrine of free will, which was supposedly the defining characteristic of the Arminians who dominated the Restoration Church of England. Writing in exile, Clarendon had branded Hobbes an opportunist. In his chapter-by-chapter refutation, *A Brief View and Survey of the Dangerous and Pernicious Errors to Church and State in Mr. Hobbes's Book, Entitled Leviathan* (1676), he claimed that Hobbes himself had told him that the purpose of *Leviathan* was to get Hobbes readmitted to England. John Wallis claimed that the purpose of *Leviathan* was to ingratiate Hobbes with Cromwell. Hobbes observed that he could hardly have anticipated in 1651 that Cromwell, away at the wars, would emerge as a quasi-monarch. Wallis called Hobbes a traitor until Hobbes pointed out that Wallis himself had deciphered the king's messages for the Parliament's army. The truth about Hobbes's allegiances is that, while Hobbes preferred monarchy, his political theory supported any form of government; and in the 'Review and

Conclusion' of *Leviathan,* Hobbes is making the best case for the legitimacy of the Commonwealth.[21]

Notwithstanding the animosity of part of the court, Charles II was not disaffected from Hobbes. A few days after the king entered London, he saw Hobbes standing in front of his residence: 'The king espied him, put off his hat very kindly to him, and asked him how he did.' Hobbes was invited to talk with the king the next week while the king had his portrait painted by Samuel Cooper (Cowper): 'Here his majesties's favours were redintegrated [*sic*] to him, and order was given that he should have free access to his majesty, who was always much delighted in his witt and smart repartees.' The king's nickname for Hobbes was 'the bear', and he would say, 'Here comes the bear to be baited!'[22]

In addition to his enemies, Hobbes had powerful friends at court. Lord Arlington, to whom Hobbes dedicated *Behemoth,* was probably the most powerful, the king excepted. Clarendon, writing in the bitterness of exile – 'the Leisure to which God hath condemn'd me' – was irritated that Hobbes 'came frequently to the Court, where he had many Disciples'.[23]

In about 1664, Aubrey suggested that Hobbes write a treatise on law. Hobbes demurred on the grounds that he probably would not live long enough to finish such an ambitious project. Aubrey gave Hobbes a copy of Bacon's *Elements of the Law,* and this was enough, it seems, to move Hobbes to write *A Dialogue ... of the Common Laws* some time later. The foil of Hobbes's work is Edward Coke, who had maintained that the common law, not the king, was the foundation of the English constitution.

In 1666, the Great Fire of London broke out. As part of the aftermath, people tried to figure out why England was suffering fire, war and pestilence; some clergy and laymen saw the adverse judgement of God in these events. Not so primitive as to think that beating a scapegoat out of London would improve their standing with God, some of the God-fearing introduced a bill into Parliament against 'atheism, profaneness, ... and swearing'. One version of the bill prescribed confinement in 'the common gaol' and a fine for anyone 'who denies or derides the essence, persons, attributes of God the Father, Son, or Holy Ghost, given to them in the Scriptures, or the omnipotency of God in the Creation, Redemption, or Governance of the world, or who denies the divine authority of any of the canonical books contained in the Old and New Testament received in the Church of England'. A revised form of the bill of 1667 adds denial of 'the immortality of men's souls, the resurrection of the body, and the eternal rewards in Heaven or eternal torments in Hell'.[24] Although it has been claimed that *Leviathan* contained denials of almost all of them, just the opposite is true.[25] Hobbes would only have trouble believing in the immortality of the soul[26] and the eternal torments of Hell. These he could have construed in a way that he would consider true. And since he had no problems professing whatever was commanded by the authorities, he would not have been bothered by professing any of these propositions. In any case, the bill was never passed and was not discussed after August 1668. (Other bills against heterodoxy were introduced in the 1670s but not passed.)

The anti-Hobbesian animus of the establishment clergy of the Restoration also exhibited itself in marginal matters. On 12 March 1669, Daniel Scargill, a callow scholar, was expelled from the University of Cambridge for asserting 'false, seditious, and impious' opinions. They were also described as 'Heretical and Blasphemous, infamous to Christian religion, and destructive of all Government in Church and State'. In short, Scargill was a Hobbist. Scargill recanted and wanted his fellowship reinstated. Even though the king wrote on his behalf, Cambridge refused. Hobbes wrote a letter about Scargill's recantation and sent a copy of it to Sir John Birkenhead, who refused to license it for printing, allegedly in order to keep favour with the bishops. No copy of the letter survives.[27] Scholars speculate that Hobbes's letter would have been self-incriminating and evidence of his atheism or irreligion.

In the early 1660s, Hobbes carried on substantial debates with John Wallis about geometry and with Robert Boyle about experimental philosophy. Hobbes came off worst in each debate, although a powerful re-evaluation of the debate with Boyle represents Hobbes's view as quite respectable.[28] Hobbes's most salient disagreement with Wallis was over Hobbes's attempts to square the circle. One version appeared in *De Corpore.* Wallis almost immediately published a criticism of it, and Hobbes presented a revised proposal in the English translation of 1656. That version was soundly criticized again. The debate carried on at least until 1674, when Hobbes published *Principia et Problemata Aliquot Geometrica Ante Desperata, Nunc Breviter Explicata & Demonstrata.* There is an irony in Hobbes's repeated failures to see that his proofs were defective. In *Leviathan,* he wrote that no one is so stupid as not to recognize a mistake in geometry when it is pointed out to him: 'For all men by nature reason alike, and well, when they have good principles. For who is so stupid, as both to mistake in Geometry, and also to persist in it, when another detects his error to him?' (*L* 5.16). Hobbes was precisely this stupid, as Wallis pointed out in *Hobbius Heauton-Timorumenos.*

Hobbes's debate with Boyle concerned the relative importance of experimentation in science. Boyle was an empiricist. He drew his conclusions from what he observed to take place as the result of his experiments with his equipment. An important piece of his equipment was an air pump. The purpose of the air pump was to extract air from a glass bulb, so that the effects of a vacuum or near vacuum could be studied. One of these was that a dog placed in the glass globe would die a few minutes after the air was supposedly extracted. While Hobbes recognized the importance of empirical investigation, he thought that Boyle's interpretations of their experiments were often flawed. Hobbes refused to believe that a vacuum or near vacuum had been produced. He claimed that the equipment was defective, and thought that a very refined air could get through tiny cracks where the cock was inserted in the neck. His alternative explanation was that the dog died not from asphyxiation but from respiratory failure caused by a change in the motion of the air.[29]

Hobbes was arguing against what Boyle took to be an empirical result. Hobbes thought that science should begin with axioms, which expressed definitions of the key terms. With well-defined axioms, one could then deduce the rest of the science. All of these propositions, then, were supposed to be true in virtue of the meaning of their terms. Hobbes called this the 'synthetic method of science' because science was being built up out of simpler concepts. There was also an analytical method, which could begin with observation. Given a certain phenomenon, a scientist could hypothesize a possible cause for it. This hypothesis might or might not be the actual cause. What was important was the usefulness of the hypothesis to deduce other propositions, which could be verified by observation. If a hypothesis was not the correct one, it would probably fail to be useful for very many observations. Hobbes's last serious effort at science was his *Decameron Physiologicum: Or, Ten Dialogues of Natural Philosophy*, published in 1678.

In addition to the purely theoretical nature of Hobbes's debate with Wallis and Boyle, there was also a social and personal aspect to it. Both of them were members of the Royal Society, while Hobbes was not. Hobbes's reputation among the international scientific community was quite high, and for that reason he was justified in thinking that by being excluded from the society he was being treated badly. Various explanations have been given for Hobbes's ostracism. One is that his views were so different from those of the Royal Society that the members thought that there could be no compatibility between them and him. Another is that Hobbes's views were very close to those of the Royal Society, that the members knew it, and that they did not want to give more ammunition to those who thought that modern science was atheistic.[30]

The Last Years

By 1673, Hobbes was eighty-five years old. He was fairly tired of the debate with Wallis and Boyle, even though it was not yet over, so he returned to an activity of his youth, translation. He published a translation of Homer's *Odyssey*. Three years later, his translation of *The Iliad* appeared. His explanation was characteristically cheeky: 'I had nothing else to do. Why publish it? Because I thought it might take off my adversaries from showing their folly upon my more serious writings, and set them upon my verses to show their wisdom.' The translations have often been criticized. Dryden wrote that Hobbes began 'studying poetry as he did mathematics, when it was too late'.

In 1674, he had a fight with John Fell, the Dean of Christ Church, Oxford. Anthony Wood was preparing his great volume, *The History and Antiquities of the University of Oxford*, when Fell, who was sponsoring the volume, objected to Wood's favourable treatment of Hobbes. Fell rewrote part of the biography. Wood, offended by the high-handedness, notified Hobbes, who wrote a scathing letter to Fell. Fell was unmoved and instructed Wood to tell Hobbes 'that he was an old man, had one foot in the grave, that he should mind his latter end, and not trouble the world any more with his papers'.[31] Meanwhile, Hobbes had obtained permission from the king to publish a response to Fell when the volume was published. Hobbes had it distributed in coffee shops and at stationers in London and Oxford. Fell was infuriated, and inserted his reply to Hobbes at the end of *The History and Antiquities*.

Hobbes left London in 1675 and never returned. The last years of his life were spent at the Cavendish estates of Chatsworth and Hardwick Hall.[32]

Hobbes fell ill for the last time in October 1679. He suffered from 'strangury', which was a generic name for any ailment that made urination difficult or painful. When he found out that it was very unlikely that he would recover, he said that he would 'be glad to find a hole to creep out of the world at'.[33] In late November, the Cavendish family was preparing to move from Chatsworth to Hardwick Hall, which enjoyed a slightly more temperate climate. They wanted to leave the ailing Hobbes at Chatsworth, but he insisted on going with them. Wrapped in blankets, he made the ten-mile journey to Hardwick by coach.

At Hardwick, he suffered a stroke that left him speechless and paralysed on one side. He was unable to receive the eucharist in this condition. He died a week later, on Thursday, 4 December 1679. He was buried on Saturday in the chancel of the church of Hault Hucknall (also known as Ault Hucknall), which was nearby.

Hobbes's reputation as an atheist and purveyor of seditious opinions continued to grow after his death. On 21 July 1683, his books *De Cive* and *Leviathan* were condemned by the University of Oxford. To put this in perspective, however, one must remember that books by John Milton, Richard Baxter, George Buchanan and John Owen were also condemned. Some of the condemned propositions were 'All civil authority is derived originally from the people,' 'The doctrine of the Gospel concerning patient suffering of injuries is not inconsistent with violent resisting of the higher powers in case of persecution for religion' and 'King Charles the First made war upon his Parliament; and in such a case the king may not only be resisted, but he ceases to be king.'[34] Obviously, the condemnation of these propositions and others in the decree was part of the agenda of a particular political group at a time when it had the power to press its will, namely, Arminian, royalist and anti-democratic clergy of the Church of England. Charles II had recently got the better of his political opponents and as a consequence had ended the Exclusion Crisis. The Rye House Plot, which involved the planned assassination of Charles II and the Duke of York, had just been foiled. The anti-absolutist, Calvinist followers of Shaftesbury and Monmouth were in disarray. Therefore, the condemnation of Hobbes's works has political significance, and cannot be taken as a measured, judicious estimation of the content of those works.

In fact, many of Hobbes's characteristic doctrines about Christianity became part of respectable thought. Some of them took less than a century, such as the view that the essence of Christianity is the doctrine that Jesus is the Christ; others took much longer. Also, Hobbes's near identification of morality with self-interest became a theme of the

Latitudinarians. Finally, in a *Festschrift* for one of the most distinguished philosophers of religion of the late twentieth century, various Christian philosophers defended the following theses: that eternal damnation is incompatible with God's goodness, that God has no obligations to creatures and that God is subject to time.[35] Of course, they do not credit Hobbes for their inspiration.

2
POLITICAL THEORY

The Goal of Political Theory

The goal of political theory has sometimes been described as the search for the nature of government and sometimes as the search for the justification for government. The first description is more likely to be given by people sympathetic to the idea that political life is natural to human beings and by those sympathetic to the philosophies of Plato, Aristotle and their followers through the centuries. Let's call this 'the classical tradition'. (Note, however, that many sophists and Stoics held that government is not natural.) The second description is more likely to be given by people who think that political life is not natural to human beings but is in some way artificial. It is the favoured modern conception of government. Hobbes represents the first giant step forward in this tradition.[1] He challenges the classical tradition at the beginning of Chapter 1 of *De Cive*:

> The greatest part of those men who have written aught concerning commonwealths, either suppose, or require us or beg of us to believe, that man is a creature born fit for society. The Greeks call him *zoon politikon*; and on this foundation they so build up the doctrine of civil society, as if for the preservation of peace, and the government of mankind, there were nothing else necessary than that men should agree to make certain covenants and conditions together, which themselves should

> then call laws. Which axiom, though received by most, is yet certainly false; and an error proceeding from our too slight contemplation of human nature. (*DC* 1.2)

Hobbes does not distinguish between the idea that government is natural to humans and the idea that people are fit for society. Yet the ideas seem to be different. One might well argue that government is natural to human beings on the grounds that they need and desire the benefits that government would provide them and that whatever is both needed and desired by a thing is natural to it. While Hobbes would agree that humans need government, he does not think they naturally desire it. The natural passions of each person are directed towards his or her own narrow self-interest and usually interfere with desiring what is in the long-term best interests of everyone. People need to be moved to see that they ought to desire the latter. This is the principal function of education.[2]

Hobbes has both theoretical and empirical arguments against the position that humans are 'born apt for society' or 'born fit for society'. One of his theoretical arguments depends upon his psychological egoism.

Psychological Egoism

According to Hobbes, every human being acts for his own good (*L* 14.8). He sometimes means that each person acts exclusively from the motive of seeking only what he perceives to be his or her own good. This position, however, is wholly unconvincing. There are simply too many examples of people helping other people. Even if people were always to act in order to gain some benefit for themselves, it would not erase the fact that sometimes they are also acting for the benefit of someone else. In other places, Hobbes expresses his egoism in a way that has no sting at all. He defines 'good' as being desired by someone, so his claim that everyone acts for his own good means only that everyone acts to satisfy his own desire. Since many people desire to help other people, what is good for many people is to help others. Therefore Hobbes's view appears to be innocuous. Scholars are divided about whether Hobbes's considered opinion is that of the radical egoist, the benign egoist, or both. The strongest case for a view in a Hobbesian spirit has been given by Gregory Kavka. He argues for 'predominant egoism', the view that 'self-interested motives tend to take precedence over non-self-interested motives in determining human actions'.[3]

Given that each human being acts only for his own good (and modest assumptions about the number of humans and some scarcity), it is plausible that humans are not naturally fit for society in the sense that they will fight with each other unless they are restrained: 'We do not therefore by nature seek society for its own sake, but that we may receive some honour or profit from it ...' (*DC* 1.2). Furthermore, human beings acting as individuals cannot curb or protect themselves from the conflicts that arise from egoistic behaviour, at least not for very long. If people are to be redeemed from their natural predicament, some other entity – possibly one created by themselves – will have to save them.

Equality

Another theoretical argument for the inevitability of war in the state of nature (that is, a condition in which individuals are not protected by laws) combines egoism with two other important Hobbesian concepts: equality and aggression. According to Hobbes, when both physical strength and native intelligence are taken together, human beings in the state of nature are equal with respect to their ability to preserve their life. About those who think that such natural equality is incredible, Hobbes says that their belief is the result of 'a vain conceit of one's own wisdom, which almost all men think they have in a greater degree than the vulgar, that is, than all men but themselves' (*L* 13.2). In fact, it can be shown that humans are equal enough for Hobbes's purposes. It does not take much intelligence and strength for a person to devise and carry out a plan to wait until someone falls asleep and then to smash his or her brains out with a rock or some other primitive weapon. Alternatively, a person who is naturally much stronger and more clever than most other people can be killed by a temporary 'confederation' of people who want to do away with him. In the American West of the nineteenth century, where institutional justice was rare and unreliable, a pistol was called 'the great equalizer'. There was also an adage: 'God made men, and Sam Colt made them equal.' If killing seems to be the obsession of this paragraph, the reason is that self-preservation is the predominant desire of human beings. That view is plausible to the extent that self-preservation is a necessary condition for all satisfactions and pleasures. Critics often charge that Hobbes overestimates the importance of the right to self-preservation to justify his philosophy. But the right to self-defence, which every political theorist recognizes, seems itself to be justified by the right of self-preservation. It is unfortunate that Hobbes did not defend his principle by making this connection more prominent.

More Causes of War

Let's return to the matter of deducing the consequences of psychological egoism and human equality, as Hobbes sees them. He holds that since people are equally able, they have the same hope of getting what they desire (*L* 13.3). His inference is invalid. Given equal strength, each person has an equal chance of fulfilling his or her desires, if all other things were equal. But all other things are not equal. Expectations affect chances of success. Some people are optimists and will believe that their chances of success are greater than those of other people; some are pessimists and will believe that their chances are less. Since optimism and pessimism come in degrees, these gradations introduce further differences. Also, the bases for optimism and pessimism may differ: some believe in luck or fate; some are courageous and some are cowardly;

some misvalue their own strength. In *Behemoth*, Hobbes says that one advantage that the Parliamentary forces had over the royalists was 'spite', which made them fight harder. (So which emotion may affect an outcome is unpredictable.)

These criticisms score points against what Hobbes actually says, but they do not destroy his view, because there are easy ways to defend it. Scarcity is the key. Under conditions of scarcity – and some scarcity has always been part of the human condition for most people – the supply of things that people want will be less than the supply needed to satisfy them all: 'And therefore if any two men desire the same thing, which nevertheless they cannot both enjoy, they become enemies' (*L* 13.4). In short, competition begets war. One of Hobbes's earliest critics, Robert Filmer, the champion of patriarchalism, denied that scarcity was a part of the human condition: 'Indeed if such a multitude of men should be created as the earth could not well nourish, there might be cause for men to destroy one another rather than perish for want of food. But God was no such niggard in the creation, and there being plenty of sustenance and room for all men, there is no cause or use of war till men be hindered in the preservation of life.'[4] My guess is that Filmer was blinded by his theological commitments.

Competition among people gives rise to 'diffidence', that is, one person's distrust of other people. Once a person possesses something in the sense of controlling its use (not in the sense of legal ownership), he must fear that other people will try to take it away from him. This fear makes it rational not only to expect the attacks of other people but also to launch pre-emptive attacks on others, because it is a poor strategy simply to wait for assaults: 'this is no more than his own conservation requires, and is generally allowed' (*L* 13.4).

A third cause of war is the propensity of some people to take 'pleasure in contemplating their own power in the acts of conquest, which they pursue farther than their security requires' (*L* 13.4). History is full of stories of people who conquered others for the mere glory of it. This same kind of behaviour would be conducted on a small scale by the same kind of people if there were no government. Hobbes then speaks more generally of all people. Everyone wants every other person to value him as much as he values himself and will do anything necessary to gain the respect he thinks he deserves, consistent with his own self-preservation. In short, 'men have no pleasure ... in keeping company where there is no power able to over-awe them all' (*L* 13.5).

There are then 'three principal causes' of war, according to Hobbes's *ex professo* account: competition, diffidence and glory. Although he gives the impression that these are separate causes, diffidence seems to presuppose and exacerbate competition, rather than being independent of it. If this is correct, then there are only two independent causes of war in his *ex professo* account. But we should not forget the other explanations for war that were mentioned earlier: equality, egoism and the desire for self-preservation. Hobbes's thought is complicated and cannot be simplified without falsifying it (*DC* 1.4). However, some scholars have tried to reduce Hobbes's complex view about the causes of war to one or two. Although these simplifications serve the interests of political theory much better than historical understanding, at least one deserves some mention.

Jean Hampton thinks that Hobbes presents two arguments. According to one, the 'rationality' account, it is rational to make war on other people, because one enhances one's chances of survival in the state of nature by doing so. According to the other, the 'passions' account, war is inevitable because people cannot control the passions that lead to war, such as the desire for glory. Hampton criticizes Hobbes; she thinks that neither argument individually is cogent and that jointly they are inconsistent. However, she thinks a Hobbesian hybrid argument is very powerful. Since most people are short-sighted, their acquisitive desires will cause war. But some people who are rational will see the long-term benefits of co-operation and will form a civil state.[5]

War and the State of Nature

The natural condition of human beings, then, is a condition of war. The usual picture of war is of two armies locked in bloody combat. Hobbes wants to repaint that picture. Combat may be described as 'hot war', but there are also cold wars of the sort that occupied the United States of America and the Soviet Union after the Second World War. Even though hardly a bullet or missile was fired by one side against the other, the USA and the USSR were genuinely at war, Hobbes would hold, because each side had an inclination to attack and to defend against the other and believed that the other had the same inclination (*L* 13.8).

Intuitively, it seems that peace has a logical priority over war. If the two are to be defined in a way that represents the relationship between them, it would seem that war is the absence of peace. This would be an especially attractive way to proceed for philosophers who thought of humans as naturally good and peace as the natural condition of humans. Hobbes, of course, does not. Since he maintains that war is part of the natural condition of human beings (a condition in which 'every man is enemy to every man'), 'war' is logically prior to peace. Consequently, he takes war as the logically prior term and defines peace as the time when people are not at war (*L* 13.8). There then follows a passage that it is almost obligatory to quote:

> In such condition, there is no place for industry; because the fruit thereof is uncertain; and consequently no culture of the earth; no navigation, nor use of the commodities that may be imported by sea; no commodious building; no instruments of moving, and removing such things as require much force; no knowledge of the face of the earth; no account of time; no arts; no letters; no society; and which is worst of all, continual fear, and danger of violent death and the life of man, solitary, poor, nasty, brutish, and short. (*L* 13.9)

Thus far in *Leviathan*, Hobbes thinks that he has given a theoretical proof of the proposition that war is the natural condition of human beings. Anticipating that some readers will remain unconvinced by an abstract argument, he appeals to experience. He claims that the fact that people travel with weapons, that they lock their doors at night and that they hide their valuables, even in their own house (in order to protect their belongings from their servants and their own children), shows that all people 'accuse mankind' by their actions (*L* 13.10). This example is revealing, but not in the way that Hobbes intends it.

His implication that the ordinary cautious behaviour of people verifies that everyone suspects everyone else of aggressive feelings is not correct. The cautious person does not think that everyone is intent on taking his belongings, nor that everyone has an inclination to harm him. Rather, the cautious person believes (1) that some people are intent on harming him and that (2) he does not know which ones these people are. From (1) and (2), it does not follow that everyone believes that everyone is out to harm them. Only the radical paranoid has that opinion. Rather, what does follow is that everyone needs to be suspicious of everyone else because some people are dangerous. This argument, which I call the 'Great Danger and Ignorance Argument', is very powerful. In contemporary society, various groups adapt it to special circumstances. Many women fear all men because some men are rapists and they do not know which they are. Children are taught to fear every stranger because some strangers are molesters, and they can never be sure which they are. Policemen are taught to be suspicious of everyone they stop for a traffic offence because some are dangerous felons, and they cannot be sure which they are. Mutual suspicion is compounded because each person knows that everyone else is suspicious of him or her. Such suspicion alerts everyone to the possibility that the others may launch pre-emptive attacks on them. This in turn causes further suspicion (*DC* Preface, 3; *L* 13.11).

The Logical Character of the State of Nature

Many people consider Hobbes's description of the state of nature to be completely implausible, especially if they think of it as a historical claim about the primeval condition of human beings. It should not be. As Hobbes says, he does not think that the state of nature ever existed 'over all the world' (*L* 13.11). The state of nature needs to be considered in two ways. First, it is an essential part of a thought experiment; that is, it should be considered a hypothetical case. Hobbes is trying to identify what the nature of human beings is, and to do this he needs to 'think away' everything that is not part of what a human being is in itself. As Hobbes understands this project, it means thinking about how human beings would act if they were not constrained by laws. When he first introduces the idea of the state of nature (or 'the natural condition of mankind') he gives the impression that there are no laws of any kind. (This has been called the 'primary state of nature'.) We have seen that he thinks that such a hypothetical situation entails that everyone would be an enemy to everyone else. He then adds to the idea of the state of nature the idea of the laws of nature, the first of which dictates that people seek peace. But these laws in themselves are ineffective; so enmity would continue in this so-called 'secondary state of nature'.[6]

The second way to consider the state of nature is not part of a thought experiment. Hobbes thinks that there are three actual kinds of situations in which part of humanity is in a state of nature. One is the condition that primitive people are in. Displaying a sorry ignorance about native Americans, Hobbes says that 'the people in many places of America' are in the state of nature (*L* 13.11). A second kind of situation is when people are in the middle of a civil war. In such a case, there is no government with the power to protect its people adequately (*L* 13.13). Hobbes was personally most worried about this sort of situation because of his knowledge of the English Civil War. The third kind of situation is that in which governments find themselves in international relations. Each national government is at war with every other national government, because there is no entity that has the power necessary to enforce laws.

Why Equality?

There may be several reasons why Hobbes wants to hold that everyone is equal in the state of nature. One is that if people are not equal, then some people are more naturally rulers or have a better claim to rule than others; and if such people exist, then they ought to be identified and recognized for their superiority. Robert Filmer's theory of patriarchy asserts a natural superiority of rulers; and there was a general opinion in the seventeenth century – Hobbes notes that it is Aristotle's view – that some people were naturally superior to others; kings and princes were superior to lords, lords to burghers and yeomen, and they in turn to labourers. Hobbes knows that there is no more chance of success in getting people to agree about who is naturally superior than there is in finding the Holy Grail. Human vanity will inspire many people to present themselves as natural-born leaders. All of these pretenders will cause war. Another reason may be that Hobbes wants to convey that the English nobility are inherently no better than the commoners and owe their high station to the sovereign, to whom they should be abjectly grateful and hence loyal. Lord Clarendon was particularly offended by this sentiment: 'In the meantime he must not take it ill that I observe his extreme malignity to the nobility by whose bread he has been always sustained, who must not expect any part, at least any precedence in his Institution.'[7]

Game Theory and the Prisoner's Dilemma

We have already alluded to the efforts of some scholars, especially political theorists and philosophers, to try to schematize Hobbes's thought. The favourite device for this project begins with what is known as the Prisoner's Dilemma, the point of which is to show that sometimes rationality and self-interest seem to conflict. Suppose that two people have been arrested for some crime. They are separated and have no way of communicating or knowing how the other person will behave. The police present each prisoner with the same proposition. If neither prisoner testifies against the other, then each will get three years in jail. (There are independent ways to convict each of something.) If only one prisoner testifies against his partner, then the one testifying will get one year in jail and the partner will get ten years. If each prisoner testifies against his partner, then each gets seven years in jail.[8] These possibilities ('outcomes') are represented in the following table ('matrix'). The two people are designated by 'A' and 'B':

		B	
		Testify	Do not
A	Testify	7, 7	1, 10
	Do not	10, 1	3, 3

The best outcome for both prisoners, taken together, is for neither to testify. Each would serve three years in jail. The worst outcome for either prisoner, considering only his own condition, is not to testify against his partner and to have the partner testify against him. (Such an outcome would put him in jail for ten years.) What causes the dilemma to arise is that a prisoner does better, relative to his partner, by testifying against him. There are two possibilities here. First, if the partner testifies against the prisoner and the prisoner also testifies, then the prisoner gets a sentence of only seven years, as against ten if he does not. Second, if the partner does not testify against the prisoner, then if the prisoner does testify against the partner, the prisoner gets a sentence of only one year as against three. Consequently, whether or not the partner testifies, each prisoner does better for himself if he testifies. What is paradoxical about this situation is that since both people (prisoner and partner) can go through the same reasoning, both will testify; both will be sentenced to seven years and thus be worse off than if both of them had not testified. The upshot of the dilemma is that group rationality is different from individual rationality.

People in the state of nature are supposed to be in a situation analogous to those described by the Prisoner's Dilemma. If each person is trying to maximize only his own interests, then everybody is worse off than if they co-operated and looked out for the interests of the whole group. The way to achieve this co-operation is by establishing a civil government. Of course, the situation in the state of nature is much more complicated than that represented by the Prisoner's Dilemma. First, there are many more people in the state of nature. Second, a rational person's strategy about how to behave in the state of nature will be affected by the fact that any decision will have consequences for how that person will be treated by the 'partner' in the future. Unless the partner dies in jail, he will have to be faced ten years down the road. Third, a rational person's strategy about how to behave in the state of nature will also be affected by the fact that any decision will have consequences for how that person will be treated by other people. If a person gets off with a one-year sentence because he testified against his partner, other people will know that he cannot be trusted and will treat him badly. Fourth, people in the state of nature can communicate with each other, while the prisoners cannot. Fifth, people in the state of nature can make promises and covenants, while the prisoners cannot. There are ways of complicating the models to take some, but perhaps not all, of these elements into account.[9]

Hobbes considers the objection that there are situations in which one's purely self-interested behaviour will not be detected and thus would be the rational course of action. This is related to Hobbes's well-known objection of the fool, the person who says that there is no justice and who professes that one need not keep his word when it is to his advantage not to. Hobbes does not accept the fool's position: the fool is a fool. Part of Hobbes's reply to him is that, since one can never be certain whether or not one's bad behaviour will be detected, it is irrational to rely upon the hope that it will not be discovered. Another part of it is that anyone professing what the fool does can expect no help from anyone else in the state of nature; yet such confederations (temporary alliances) are necessary for survival (*L* 14.4).

Some of the problems with explicating Hobbes's views with the devices of game theory have been mentioned above. In short, Hobbes's thought is complex, and the models are either too simple or so complex that their value to illuminate the issues is greatly diminished. Also, Hobbes does not always follow the most logical or straightforward path through a problem. To the extent that he introduces something *ad hoc* or includes elements that are not or cannot be included, the value of the model diminishes. For example, the fool's objection has to do with the relationship between reason and justice, not with reason alone, as the Prisoner's Dilemma does. A related objection is that Hobbes is not concerned with the problem of maximizing utilities, but with self-preservation: 'The twentieth-century obsession with the "prisoner's dilemma" and with the temptation to be a "free-rider" presupposes a theory of motivation that Hobbes did not believe in. What Hobbes's individuals maximize in the state of nature is *power.*'[10]

Finally, game theory modelling also decontextualizes Hobbes's text. For those who care that Hobbes is commenting on various historical events, such as those who violated the oath of the Solemn League and Covenant by taking the Engagement Oath, game theory is either unilluminating or distorting.[11]

The Right of Nature

Since the natural condition of human beings is one in which there is either no law at all or at least no effective law, the behaviour of human beings is not constrained in any way; in other words, they have a right to everything.[12] At its first mention, the right of nature is defined as 'the liberty each man has to use his own power, as he will himself, for the preservation of his own nature, that is to say, his own life; and consequently, of doing any thing which in his own judgment and reason he shall conceive to be the aptest means thereto' (*L* 14.1). Three components of this definition should be noted: (1) the right of nature is a liberty or freedom to act; (2) its goal is self-preservation; and (3) each person must judge for him- or herself how to achieve that goal. Presented in this way, the right of nature is a plausible principle. Later, however, Hobbes in effect drops component (2) and asserts that by the right of nature 'every man has a right to every thing, even to one another's body' (*L* 14.4). This simplified version of the right of nature is implausible, and it is not obvious how it follows from the original. The original version justifies taking only those things that contribute to one's own self-preservation, whatever they may be. It does not justify control or possession of all that exists. If a person were hungry and there was no food available other than the flesh of another human being, then the original principle would justify eating that person. But the principle justifies cannibalism only in these extreme circumstances. If a person needs the equivalent of a loaf of bread to survive, and both an ample supply of bread and a human being are available, the original version of the right of nature does not justify ignoring the bread and eating the human being; but the second does.

Why, then, does Hobbes revise the idea of the right of nature by dropping (2)? There are two reasons. One is rhetorical. Without (2), the state of nature is made all the more horrible and dangerous; in it 'there can be no security to any man ... of living out the time which nature ordinarily allows men to live' (*L* 14.4). The other is philosophical. Since there is no authority to decide disagreements in the state of nature, no one can definitively deny that another person has the right to anything that that person tries to acquire. Even though there is an objective truth about whether or not a certain course of action contributes to preserving a person's life, since there is no institutional judge in the state of nature, no one's opinion has any force with respect to the behaviour of another person. Consequently, the rights of each person are in effect unrestricted, as the revised version of the right of nature asserts.

The Means of Getting Out of the State of Nature

The state of nature is wretched; it is a condition that one should want to get out of as quickly as possible. What is it within the human being that permits this escape? Hobbes says it lies 'partly in the passions, partly in his [man's] reason'. Fear of death and the desire for a comfortable life are the motives for getting out of the state of nature; the hope that people can have a decent life through hard work and the use of reason are the means by which it can happen (*L* 13.14). Reason leads one to the laws of nature.

The Law of Nature

Hobbes has slightly different definitions of 'law of nature' in *De Cive* and *Leviathan*. In the earlier work, he says a law of nature is 'a dictate of right reason' about what should be done or avoided in order to preserve one's life and health (*DC* 2.1). For Hobbes, every genuine law has to have a lawgiver, and he gives the clear impression in *De Cive* that reason itself plays this role for the laws of nature. Since reason, not being a person, cannot literally be a lawgiver, the laws of nature cannot literally be laws. Thus a majority of scholars conclude that, for Hobbes, the laws of nature are not genuine laws but rather prudential maxims. The laws of nature, on this interpretation, instruct humans about the best way to escape the state of nature. Whether the laws of nature as prudential maxims can count as moral considerations is typically considered to be a separate issue.

Most scholars think that Hobbes never changed his views about the laws of nature; but it is arguable that the account in *Leviathan* is different. There he defines a law of nature as (1) a precept or general rule, (2) discovered by reason, and (3) by which a person is forbidden to do something that destroys his life or not to do something that preserves it (*L* 14.3). Component (1) in effect expresses the genus to which the laws of nature belong. There are two kinds of precepts: those that one is obliged to follow (laws and commands) and those that one is not obliged to follow (counsels). In subsequent chapters, Hobbes insists that the sovereign – he has in mind the monarch – may receive counsel from advisors – he has in mind a parliament – but not commands. Component (2) indicates the way in which a law is promulgated. People must use their reason to figure out what the laws of nature are; in contrast, people must listen to the commands of their sovereign to find out what the civil laws are. Component (3) specifies the scope or content of the laws of nature: self-preservation.

Component (3) also mentions that certain behaviour is 'forbidden' by the laws of nature. This raises the question, 'Who forbids it?' Hobbes's remark that 'everyone is governed by his own reason' suggests that reason does the forbidding. On this interpretation, then Hobbes's view is the same in *De Cive* and *Leviathan*: the term, 'laws of nature' is metaphorical; and the laws of nature are in fact not laws but prudential precepts or, as some hold, 'assertoric hypothetical imperatives' – that is, propositions that prescribe means to a given end.[13]

What counts against this interpretation is (a) the fact that Hobbes takes a strong stand against using words metaphorically in philosophy; (b) his numerous remarks to the effect that God commands the laws of nature and is their author; and (c) his categorization of the laws of nature as one kind of law, along with divine positive laws and civil laws. If the laws of nature were laws only metaphorically, then they would no more belong in a categorization of laws than computer bugs would belong in a taxonomy of insects.

There are also numerous passages that strongly suggest that the laws of nature are genuine laws. For example, Hobbes sometimes indicates that previous thinkers were confused in their use of the term 'the laws of nature'. Hobbes holds that a law has two parts: a part that expresses what is to be done or avoided (that is, the content of the law) and a part that expresses the authority by which the law is made (that is, its form). In a law such as 'I command that each person pay one month's salary to the government,' the phrase 'I command' expresses the form, and the rest of the sentence expresses the content. Clarifying the nature of laws of nature, Hobbes maintains that the content of the laws of nature is deducible by reason. This part of the laws may be called 'dictates of reason'. According to Hobbes, many thinkers 'used to call' them laws 'but improperly; for they are but conclusions or theorems concerning what conduces to the conservation and defence of themselves ...' Since Hobbes is talking about what they used to be improperly called, it is unlikely that he thinks that his own use of the term 'law of nature' is improper. This is confirmed by what he says next: 'But yet if we consider the same theorems, as delivered in the word of God, that by right commands all things, then are they properly called laws' (*L* 15.41; 26.3). Earlier, God's role in the laws of nature was indicated when Hobbes refused to hold that oaths (that is, promises in which the name of God is used to signify the guarantor) have any more force than covenants, in which God's name is not invoked: 'For a covenant, if lawful, binds in the sight of God, without the oath, as much as with it: if unlawful, binds not at all; though it be confirmed with an oath' (*L* 14.33). Since it is the laws of nature that are being discussed, the law that binds in the sight of God must be the law of nature. So, it is arguable that Hobbes changed his view about the laws of nature, from being prudential precepts (in *De Cive*) to being genuine laws commanded by God (in *Leviathan*). But this remains a minority interpretation.

There is also a philosophical problem with attributing to Hobbes the view that the laws of nature are merely prudential: they seem to lack force. There is no moral failing in doing the imprudent thing, and no obligation is violated. It is easy to think of circumstances in which the benefit of breaking a covenant is very great and the probability of being discovered is very low, while the possible harm that would come from keeping the covenant is also very great. In such cases, rationality would seem to dictate breaking the covenant, and Hobbes would have no convincing response unless covenants were backed by an omnipotent God.

The First Law of Nature

In *De Cive,* Hobbes formulates 'the first and fundamental law of nature' as 'that peace is to be sought after, where it may be found out, and where not, there to provide ourselves for helps of war'. In *Leviathan,* Hobbes calls the proposition that corresponds to this 'a precept or general rule of reason'; and only the first part of it expresses the first or fundamental law of nature. That is, the first law of nature is: that every person ought to seek peace, to the extent that he or she has a hope of securing it. The rest of the precept or general rule of reason is 'the sum of the right of nature': that where peace is not possible, a person should wage war in order to defend him- or herself (*DC* 2.2; *L* 14.4). It is possible that Hobbes split the proposition in this way in order to have 'the right of nature' do more work in *Leviathan.* (The right of nature is not as prominent in *De Cive.*)

The Second Law of Nature

All the other laws of nature are supposed to follow from the first. The second law is that a person should be willing 'to lay down this right to all things' so long as others are willing to lay down the same (*L* 14.5; *DC* 2.3). One way to derive this law from the first is by *reductio ad absurdum.* Suppose that a person is not willing to lay down this right to all things. Then the person will be making no effort towards peace, since the right to all things is one of the causes of war. Since this consequence contradicts the first law of nature, the assumption of the *reductio* must be false. *Q.E.D.*

An Ambiguity in 'The Right to All Things'

According to the second law of nature, people need to lay down their rights to all things. Renouncing their rights would not guarantee their safety. It is only by transferring their rights, and hence their power, to some entity (the sovereign) that they can benefit from the loss of rights. The phrase 'to lay down their right to all things' is ambiguous. It can mean (A) that they lay down some of their rights with the consequence that they no longer have a right to everything, or it can mean (B) that they lay down every right with the consequence that they would end up with no rights at all. On the one hand, interpretation (A) is a sensible requirement to place on people instituting a government. If Hobbes means (A) his premise is plausible, and his readers will be inclined to accept it. Hobbes seems to mean (A) when he first introduces it (*EL* 1.17.2; *DC* 5.7). However, (A) is not strong enough to justify the unrestricted kind of government at which Hobbes aims. On the other hand, (B) is strong enough to justify the monopoly on power that is necessary for absolute sovereignty, but is not a proposition that people would be eager to accept as a condition for government. Hobbes seems to subscribe to (B) when he discusses the formula for establishing a government.[14] The requirement that people 'confer all their power and strength upon one man or assembly of men' (*L* 17.13) is a consequence of (B).[15]

Covenants

The third law of nature is that a person is willing to keep his covenants when others are willing to do the same. Like the second, it can be proved by a *reductio*. If a person were not willing to keep his covenants, then he would not be willing to make peace. To make a covenant is to lay down a right in a specific way.

Laying Down of Rights

The ideas of laying down, renouncing and transferring rights are central to Hobbes's discussion of the formation of government. According to Hobbes, governments are established by covenants. This is what makes him a social contract theorist. To enter into a covenant is to lay down a right to something in order to gain something else. Hobbes distinguishes two ways in which a right can be laid down. A right can be renounced or transferred. To renounce a right is not to exercise it and not to care who benefits from that action. For example, if ten people have a right to take apples from a tree and one person renounces his right, then the other nine people increase their chances of getting the apples by about 10 per cent. Hobbes does not have any intrinsic interest in the idea of renouncing a right. It is useful primarily in the contrast that it provides for the idea of transferring a right. Hobbes says that to transfer a right is to 'intend the benefit thereof to some certain person or persons' (*L* 14.7). Doing so creates an obligation not to interfere with those to whom the right has been transferred. Although Hobbes is not always clear about it, to transfer a right to someone sometimes requires contributing one's power to that person for the purpose of having that person possess or maintain the object. This is especially important when one transfers one's right of governing oneself to the sovereign. But it also applies to the trivial case of transferring one's right to the apples. The transfer requires that the granter do something to help that person take possession of them. Selling an object to a person is an act of transferring a right to that thing; and handing the object over to the other person is sufficient to help the person possess it.

Sovereign-making Covenants

Let's now consider the relationship between sovereign-making covenants and the transfer of rights. One of the most perplexing features of Hobbes's political philosophy is the explicit formula that Hobbes thinks expresses the essence of establishing a sovereign: 'I authorize and give up my right of governing myself to this man, or to this assembly of men, on this condition, that thou give up thy right to him, and authorize all his actions in like manner' (*L* 17.13). In order to understand the issues here, it is helpful to introduce a distinction between two ways in which the authority of a sovereign is explained.

Authorization and Alienation

According to one of these ways, people authorize their sovereign to act for them in matters concerning public safety. To put this more formally: a person *x* authorizes a person *y* exactly when *x* chooses *y* to act for *x*. According to the other, people alienate their rights to their sovereign, who then has a free hand in making decisions about how they are to be governed. That is, *x* alienates a right *R* to a person *y* exactly when *x* gives up *R* to *y* and cannot recover it unilaterally. A non-political example of alienating a right is selling something. The right to an object that has been sold is recoverable by re-purchase (which implies the consent of the new owner), or by a gift of the new owner, or by abandonment by the new owner. None of these methods involves a unilateral act on the part of the person who alienated her right.

Authorization and alienation seem to be incompatible. Authorization is unilaterally revocable and does not involve laying down any right. But alienation is not unilaterally revocable and is a way of laying down a right. The problem for interpreters of Hobbes is that he appears to subscribe to both authorization and alienation.[16] His theory of alienation is easy to see in the part of the sovereign-making formula that reads, 'I ... give up my right of governing myself to this man or to this assembly of men ...' This follows upon his explanation that the only way for people to defend themselves effectively is 'to confer all their power and strength upon one man or upon one assembly of men' (*L* 17.13). This passage seems clearly to assert that the subject has alienated all of his rights. However, there are other passages that appear inconsistent with the 'alienation' clause of the sovereign-making formula. Hobbes had said that there are some rights that 'no man can be understood by any words, or other signs, to have abandoned or transferred'. Some of these include the right not to be wounded or imprisoned. Because these rights cannot be laid down, a prisoner, especially one condemned to death, has the right to resist his executioners. Thus, no one can lay down all their rights by taking the sovereign-making covenant, even if the words give that impression: 'And therefore if a man by words or other signs seem to despoil himself of the end for which those signs were intended, he is not to be understood as if he meant it or that it was his will' (*L* 14.8). While it is very sensible for Hobbes to hold that no one can lay down all of his rights, it creates a problem with respect to the proper interpretation of the sovereign-making formula. If a person does not give up all of his or her rights, then one wants to know which ones or how many of them he or she does give up. A sensible approach to government – but this is not Hobbes's – would be to hold that one should give up just as many rights as is necessary to create a government strong enough to ensure domestic tranquillity and safety against foreign invasion, but not so many that one gives up those that are very important to happiness, such as the right to privacy, worship, free speech and assembly. In short, government would not be absolutely sovereign, as Hobbes understands it, because it would not have theoretical control over every aspect of life. According to Hobbes, government has to be absolutely sovereign in the sense of having a monopoly on all the political power in the state and the right to regulate every aspect of human life, in order to maintain stability (see below). Hobbes reassures his readers that no sovereign would in fact control every aspect of human life because they lack the practical power to do so (*L* 21.6). While liberty in the state of nature was unlimited, liberty in the civil state is restricted to those things that are not prohibited by law.

Hobbes's commitment to a theory of authorization comes out in that part of the sovereign-making formula that reads, 'I authorize ... this man or ... this assembly of men ... and authorize all his actions in like manner.' According to Hobbes, when people in the state of nature set up a sovereign, they thereby create an artificial person, who acts for them ('bears their person') (*L* 17.13). According to Hobbes, a natural person is one whose voluntary behaviour counts as his or her own actions. In contrast, an artificial person is one whose behaviour counts as the actions of someone else. The artificial person is called the 'actor' and the person to whom the action is attributed is called the 'author'. Thus, citizens are the authors of the actions of the sovereign, who is nothing but an actor (*L* 16). This view has the advantage of attributing the responsibility for all of the policies of the sovereign to the subjects themselves. Hobbes proverbially wants his sovereign to have his cake and eat it too. The sovereign, according to Hobbes, has the sole authority for decision-making and yet is unaccountable to his subjects for those decisions. Those decisions are technically the actions of the subjects themselves, whether they like them or not.

Hobbes was not making a purely theoretical point. He was galled by the execution of Charles and makes a dig at the regicides: 'no man that has sovereign power can justly be put to death, or otherwise in any manner by his subjects punished. For seeing every subject is author of the actions of his sovereign, he punishes another for the actions committed by himself' (*L* 18.7). In short, Charles was a scapegoat for the regicides. Those who accept Clarendon's view that Hobbes wrote *Leviathan* in order to assuage the leaders of the Commonwealth need to explain how this and other passages like it are consonant with their view (e.g. *L* 18.16).

When it suits his purposes to make the sovereign the author and the subjects merely actors, he does not hesitate to take that line. For example, Hobbes holds that the sovereign is the ultimate religious authority, as well as the ultimate secular authority, in the civil state. Thus, the religion of the sovereign is the religion of the people. To the objection that Christians are not permitted to worship in a pagan fashion even if ordered to do so by the sovereign, Hobbes denies that such ritual behaviour would count as the actions of the Christians at all. He claims that it is not the Christians at all who are at worship, despite all appearances to the contrary. Their behaviour, which is subject to the commands of their sovereign, counts as the worship of the sovereign only. The subjects are merely actors in the ritual; the sovereign is the author of it.

What Hobbes says about authorization seems to mean that a subject authorizes everything that the sovereign does. But such an unrestricted authorization is as offensive and implausible as the unrestricted alienation of rights that was discussed above. Even if the authorization is restricted to the sovereign's governance, there is a difficult problem to solve. If the subjects authorize the sovereign, why cannot the subjects de-authorize him? If a person authorizes someone to buy a house for him and becomes dissatisfied with the agent's handling of the matter, that person can terminate the authorization either immediately or at least after some contractually specified time. The important point is that the authorization is revocable. In contrast, Hobbes says that subjects cannot revoke their authorization, and he would appeal to his theory of alienation to justify that position. The question is whether authorization and alienation can coherently coexist, and I have suggested that they cannot.

Rhetorically, Hobbes needs to have both authorization and alienation. If people authorize their sovereign, then they have acted freely to have the sovereign represent them and therefore do not have the right to complain. As Hobbes explains authorization, the behaviour of the sovereign does not count as his own actions but as the actions of the subjects who authorized him. Concerning alienation, if people alienate their rights to the sovereign, then they cannot regain them. This ensures political stability on a theoretical level at least. (In this regard, Locke was probably right when he made the general point that theories do not make a government more or less stable as a matter of fact.) Concerning how much power or authority a sovereign has, Hobbes equivocates, as I have indicated above. Sometimes he indicates that because subjects have given up their right to everything, the sovereign has the right to control every aspect of life. But he also categorically asserts that a person can never give up his or her right to self-preservation. The equivocation is possible because of the ambiguity of the phrase 'to give up the right to all things'.

Let's consider one other problem with the phrase. (1) No matter what the sovereign-making formula seems to say, no one can give up those rights that are necessary for self-preservation: the right of resistance or the right of self-defence. (2) Whoever has a right to an end has a right to the means to that end. (3) According to Hobbes, no one can ever know what he or she may need in order to achieve the end of self-preservation. (He uses this very consideration to make the authority of the sovereign unrestricted: the sovereign could not survive if he could be second-guessed.) (1)–(3) seem to entail that no one can ever give up (alienate) any right. One must always have the right to judge what is necessary for one's own preservation. This would seem to have the further consequence that the sovereign's authority is always in potential conflict with the subject's right to self-preservation, because any action of the sovereign may affect the subject's life and hence may be construed as not having been yielded. Hobbes would abhor this consequence but, given his principles, it is not clear how he can avoid it.

Setting aside any philosophical problems that Hobbes's sovereign-making formula may contain, let's consider his view about the nature of the covenant itself. First, the parties to the covenant are the potential subjects themselves. The sovereign is not a covenanting party (*L* 18.4). Rather, each potential subject lays down his right 'of governing himself' to the sovereign. Hobbes is not always clear about what this transfer amounts to. Sometimes he gives the impression that it involves nothing more than standing aside: 'And because it is impossible for any man really to transfer his own strength to another: or for that other to receive it, it is to be understood that *to transfer a man's power and strength is no more but to lay by or relinquish his own right of resisting him* to whom he so transfereth it' (*EL* 1.19.10; see also 1.19.7). Obviously, no sovereign could govern his subjects and protect them from foreign invasion if he had to rely only upon his own strength while his subjects stood aside. The sensible way to construe this passage is to hold that 'not resisting' the sovereign involves obeying the sovereign's commands: to pay money when taxed, to take up arms when invaded, and so on. When all subjects transfer their right in this way, the sovereign acquires enormous power to protect the subjects.

According to the normal view of it, contracting parties create duties to each other. If two people contract to sell an object, then one of them creates the duty of paying the other money, and the other creates the duty of handing over the object. But, according to Hobbes, the contracting parties create an obligation not to each other but to the sovereign; specifically, the obligation of obeying all the commands of the sovereign. The sovereign has no obligation to the subjects. He does, however, have an obligation to obey the laws of nature. If the laws of nature are construed as laws of God, then the sovereign's obligation is to God. Who can judge whether the obligations to God have been fulfilled? Only God, according to Hobbes; certainly not the subjects.

Sovereignty by Institution and Sovereignty by Acquisition

Hobbes makes a distinction between two ways in which governments are created. When a government emerges from the state of nature (in which all people are equal), the sovereign is instituted by the decision of the subjects. This is known as sovereignty by institution. Hobbes deals with this method of creating a government because it most clearly reveals the logical structure of sovereignty.

However, historically most governments were not instituted but acquired by force, as William the Conqueror had acquired his sovereignty over England. This is known as sovereignty by acquisition. In conquest, the defeated people make a covenant according to which the conquering power becomes the sovereign. There are two possibilities here. First, the defeated people may covenant with each other to make the conquering power their sovereign. Since the sovereign in this case is the representative of another civil state, the resulting form of government is actually an aristocracy, in which all the people of the conquering state constitute the sovereignty. (This is admittedly a non-standard notion of aristocracy.) Second, the defeated people may covenant with the subjects of the conquering power to make that power their sovereign. In this case, the conquered subjects become incorporated into the civil state that defeated them, and the form of government is that of the conquering state, which may be either a monarchy, aristocracy or democracy.

Hobbes's treatment of sovereignty by institution and by acquisition has been much debated and criticized by scholars, largely because his treatment of sovereignty by acquisition is confused.[17] Sometimes he seems to say that the covenant that results from it is between the conquered people and the conquering power, even though the sovereign is not supposed to be a party to the covenant. Also, there is no equality at all between the conquered people and the conquering power; and this seems to undercut the importance of equality in the state of nature as a necessary condition for needing government. There is no denying that Hobbes did not present his views about sovereignty by acquisition in the best light. Nonetheless, the interpretation presented above is implicit in Hobbes's account and captures the spirit of his views.

Although scholars have tried to emphasize the difference between sovereignty by institution and sovereignty by acquisition, Hobbes minimizes it. For him, the only difference is that in the former the people who choose their sovereign 'do it for fear of one another and not of him whom they institute', while in the latter case, 'they subject themselves to him they are afraid of' (*L* 20.2). In each case, the nature of sovereignty is the same: the sovereign is absolute.[18]

Absolute Sovereignty

For Hobbes, an absolute sovereign has two properties: he has all the political power that there is in the state, and he has the right to govern every aspect of life.[19] The fact that subjects are free to behave largely as they please is a result of the fact that it is impracticable for the sovereign to make laws that cover many aspects of life. As mentioned above, Hobbes is naïve on this point.

The sovereign has properties that mimic those traditionally assigned to God. He is practically omnipotent because no one can compete with his power; he is practically omniscient because he decides what will be taken to be true in all matters of controversy. He is all just because he makes the laws, administers them and is not subject to them himself. The sovereign is also a redeemer. Redemption involves two beliefs. One is that there is something radically wrong with either people or the world. The other is that people cannot save themselves. Hobbes has already shown that there is something radically wrong with human life in the state of nature, and individual human beings cannot save themselves. Their sovereign can do it for them. Hobbes exploits the analogy between God and the sovereign: the sovereign (Leviathan) is a 'mortal god, to which we owe, under the immortal God, our peace and defence' (*L* 17.13). My guess is that Hobbes was also thinking of what James I said about kings: 'Kings are justly called gods for that they exercise a manner or resemblance of divine power upon earth. For if you will consider the attributes of God, you shall see how they agree in the person of a king.'[20]

Top-down and Bottom-up Theories

Political theories can be divided into those that are top-down and those that are bottom-up.[21] According to top-down theories, political legitimacy originates at the highest level of authority and filters down to lower orders. Patriarchalism and the theory of the divine right of kings are examples. According to bottom-up theories, political legitimacy originates from the subjects or citizens themselves and is transferred to entities that thereby acquire authority. 'Democracy' is the name of both a political theory and a form of government; and they should not be confused. As a political theory, democracy is a bottom-up one. Political authority originates with the people, who institute a form of government. As a form of government, democracy can be given a top-down justification. Suppose that patriarchalism is the correct theory of government. Nothing prevents the patriarch from choosing a democratic form of government as the method by which the people will be governed. (The patriarch could also choose an aristocratic or even a monarchical form.) Another top-down justification for democracy could be called 'a divine right of democracy' theory, according to which all authority originates with God, and He then transfers some authority to the people as a whole. Samuel Rutherford in *Lex Rex* (1644) held a theory like this.

As a matter of historical fact, top-down theories have been more likely to defend the doctrine of absolute sovereignty than bottom-up ones. But there is no logical necessity for this. One of the reasons why Hobbes's political theory was bewildering to his contemporaries and is intriguing to us is that he develops a bottom-up theory for absolute sovereignty. Royalists who were absolutists despised Hobbes's democratic principles. Robert Filmer, the notorious author of *Patriarch* and an absolutist, intuited the novelty of Hobbes's doctrine. He praised Hobbes's absolutism but criticized his ideas about the state of nature.[22] Non-royalists who emphasized the limits of sovereignty despised his absolutism. Although there were budding theories of popular sovereignty during the mid-seventeenth century – for example, those of Milton, Rutherford and the Levellers – Hobbes does not seem to have been influenced by them. The reason is that all of these theorists argued for limited sovereignty.

Moral Philosophy

In its ordinary sense, virtually all of Hobbes's moral philosophy is part of his politics.[23] To the extent that ethics is concerned with human happiness, Hobbes's psychology is relevant; but to the extent that ethics is a normative science, only his politics is. For humans, happiness consists in continually satisfying desires. There is no obligation, praiseworthiness or culpability in this; it is a fact of nature. Obligation, praiseworthiness and blame arise only when there is a certain kind of law; and that law, as we have seen, belongs to political life.

Richard Tuck has argued persuasively that Hobbes's moral philosophy ought to be seen within a tradition that begins with Hugo Grotius and continues with John Selden, Hobbes, Richard Cumberland, Samuel Pufendorf and John Locke. What characterizes it is the search for a deductive science of politics that begins with propositions that are necessarily true. It is motivated by the idea that the natural right of self-preservation is the foundation for morality and that *raison d'état* is the analogue for politics. Consequently, the apparent emphasis that these writers place on natural law is misleading.[24]

Conclusion

After Hobbes died, his reputation as an atheist in religion and an absolutist in politics combined to make him a thoroughly disreputable fellow. Virtually no one referred to him positively; yet important parts of his thought were picked up by a variety of political thinkers from Spinoza to Pufendorf and Locke to Barbeyrac. Without acknowledging or perhaps even recognizing it, the Latitudinarians adopted the Hobbesian view that self-interest and morality coincide. One of the leaders of that movement, John Tillotson, wrote that 'religion and happiness, our duty and our interest are really but one and the same thing considered under several notions'.[25]

3

Religious Views

Introduction

Hobbes thought that religion was characteristic of human beings and thus could not be eliminated; he also thought that religious doctrines often destabilized government and hence needed to be controlled by the sovereign. Concerning specific concepts and issues related to religion, he believed that humans have no idea of God; spirits are bodies, subjects should obey their sovereigns in all matters except those that jeopardize salvation; and for Christians the only belief necessary for salvation is that Jesus is the Messiah.

Hobbes did not begin publishing his views about religion until 1640, at the age of fifty-two, when he circulated his manuscript, *The Elements of Law, Natural and Politic.* Only three of its twenty-nine chapters concern religion. It is possible that Hobbes does not devote more space to religion in that work because he did not think it was necessary. The excesses that he perceived in dissident religious groups, particularly the Presbyterians, had not yet been played out. The situation was quite different in 1642 when the first edition of *De Cive* appeared. The anti-establishment religious groups in Parliament had already succeeded in having Laud imprisoned and Strafford executed. So religion is conspicuous in *De Cive.* 'Of Religion' is one of the three parts into which that book is divided. (The other two are 'Of Liberty' and 'Of Dominion'.)

The importance of religion in Hobbes's thought continued to grow over the decades. At least half of *Leviathan* concerns various aspects of religion. In the 1660s, he wrote various works on religious matters. Of these latter works, the most important are *Considerations Upon the Reputation, Loyalty, Manners, and Religion of Thomas Hobbes of Malmesbury*, written in 1662, but not published until 1680, and two works written in the mid- to late 1660s, *An Historical Narration Concerning Heresy and the Punishment Thereof* (1680), and *An Answer to a Book Published by Dr. Bramhall ... called the 'Catching of the Leviathan*' (1682). Hobbes's reputation as an atheist increased from the Restoration on at least until the end of the century. However, none of his friends, who included several prominent Roman Catholic priests and many members of the Church of England, ever indicated in their public writings or private correspondence that he was an atheist. His first biographer, John Aubrey, wrote: 'For his being branded with atheism, his writings and virtuous life testify against it.'[1]

Most of those who thought that he was an atheist did not know him personally. John Bramhall did, but he knew that Hobbes was not a professed atheist. His accusation was that Hobbes's principles led to atheism. Bishop Henry Hammond may have had the same thing in mind when he called *Leviathan* a 'farrago of Christian atheism'. As part of his defence, Hobbes coined the term 'atheism by consequence'. He cautioned Bramhall against using the term, because he thought that Bramhall's principles, not his own, led to atheism. In the eighteenth century, 'Hobbism' was the word for the native species of English atheism. And if the criterion of truth is the received opinion, then Hobbes was never so much an atheist as he was during the first half of the twentieth century. The notable dissenting voice during this latter time was A. E. Taylor, who argued that Hobbes's ethical philosophy was a Kantian form of divine command theory. In the second half of the century, Howard Warrender's book on Hobbes presented the strongest case for making theism part of Hobbes's political theory, at least until the last decade.

Scholarly belief in Hobbes's irreligious beliefs or, at most, deism, remains the dominant interpretation of him.[2]

As historians and historically oriented political scientists and philosophers began to study Hobbes in the 1980s, the interpretations of Hobbes's religious views have become richer and more subtle, although the majority opinion still maintains that Hobbes was either an atheist or a deist, and that, in either case, he was intent on subverting belief in revealed religion. Many scholars would now agree that Hobbes intended his analyses of religious concepts to forestall the possibility that they could be used to destabilize government or to set limits on scientific theorizing. Nonetheless, these intentions are compatible with both belief and disbelief in Christianity.[3]

Naturalism and Theism

Hobbes is thoroughly naturalistic, in his own way. According to naturalism, the only things that exist are things in and of nature. Typically, philosophical naturalists are atheists, because most think that if God exists, then He must transcend or be outside of the physical world. Hobbes is different in that he professes that God both exists and is part of the physical world. Indeed, God is a body, because God is a substance and all substances are bodies. Hobbes maintains that the idea of an immaterial substance is a contradiction in terms and was imported from pagan, Greek philosophy. He correctly points out that the Bible never uses the term 'immaterial substance' or any equivalent. Hobbes's God might be called immanent, since it exists within the universe, but it is not the least bit anthropomorphic. Hobbes says that it cannot be literally true that God sees, hears or speaks, because 'if they were to be taken in the strict and proper sense, one might argue from his making of all parts of man's body that he had also the same use of them which we have; which would be many of them so uncomely, as it would be the greatest contumely in the world to ascribe them to him' (*L* 36.9). Sometimes Hobbes says that it is literally true to assert that God exists and that nothing else is literally true about Him. At other times, he says that God is eternal, infinite and omnipotent in a way that gives the impression that he means these things literally (*L* 12.6–7).

Hobbes is fairly consistent in maintaining that human beings cannot know what God's nature is. This is not a radical proposition at all, since Hobbes also maintains that human beings do not even know the nature of the smallest living creature (*L* 31.33). Hobbes's remark says as much about the limitations of human knowledge as it does about God. Furthermore, to say that humans cannot know the nature of God is not to say that nothing can be known about God. According to Christians, God is a creator and sent His son as a redeemer. The relational properties of being a creator and redeemer are not part of God's nature, but they can be truly attributed to Him.

Even though he had earlier restricted the literally true things that can be said about God to existence, omnipotence and infiniteness, Hobbes at one point specifies the 'attributes' of God that are 'taught us by the light of Nature' (*L* 31.14). This language suggests that the attributes that he will specify literally apply to God. This holds true for the very first claim that Hobbes makes: God exists. But then his language begins to have a different force. He says that those who said that God is the world or the soul of the world 'denied his existence' and spoke 'unworthily' of Him. This latter claim (to speak 'unworthily' of God) does not bear directly on truth or falsity. Rather, it concerns religiously appropriate language. But Hobbes then returns to a matter that does concern truth and falsity. He says that God is 'the cause of the world' and implies, but does not say, that He created the world. But he then reverts to talking about what honours and dishonours God: to say that God does not care for humans or that He is finite, has a shape, has parts, is in a place, is moved or at rest or has emotions is to 'take from Him His honour' (*L* 31.17). This is irrelevant to the truth: to say of certain people – say, politicians – that they are racists, thieves or adulterers is to take from them their honour; and yet it may be true. Since

Hobbes maintains that God is a body, God must be in some place, even though Hobbes maintains that to say this dishonours Him. Similarly, since Hobbes holds that God is the cause of everything and every cause is in motion, God must be in motion, even though Hobbes maintains that to say this also dishonours Him.

In one clear way, it is not surprising that Hobbes abandons cognitive talk about God – that is, talk that specifies what is true or false – for a discussion of laudative talk. It fits both with Hobbes's theory about religious language (to be discussed next) and his relatively uncompromising commitment to the favourite divine epithet of Calvinists, namely, that God is incomprehensible.

Honorific Religious Language

According to Hobbes, God cannot and should not be an object of scientific investigation. He should be worshipped and honoured (*L* 12.7). People should talk to God and not about God, as Martin Buber observed more than once. In the twentieth century, a number of distinguished and respectable philosophers of religion, most notably Ian Ramsey, Nolloth Professor of the Philosophy of Christian Religion at Oxford, have explained religious language in ways similar to Hobbes's.[4] Their motivation was to overcome the challenges made by scientific and linguistic theories to traditional religious belief. Hobbes seemed to recognize the very same kinds of challenges. Since modern science never appeals to God in its explanations of phenomena, God plays no role in science and becomes a useless hypothesis. According to Hobbes's linguistic views, 'God' is the name of an object of which humans can have no image. Modern science and modern linguistic theory make easy bedfellows. Religion that professes that God is incomprehensible makes a strange bedfellow, even though logically it is possible for it to sleep in the same bed.

Negative Theology

These three propositions – that God is incomprehensible, that God is not an object of science and that God cannot be sensed – led Hobbes to develop a version of 'negative theology', the view that human beings cannot say what God is like, but only what He is not like. This view had a long and respectable history; even Thomas Aquinas espoused it: 'Because we cannot know what God is, but only what He is not, we cannot consider how He is but only how He is not.'[5] For Hobbes, other than asserting His existence, humans can only truly deny that God has certain properties or speak honourably of Him. Although it is difficult to subscribe to negative theology consistently without immediately falling silent after professing it, Hobbes did better than most negative theologians. He summarized his view by saying that 'He that will attribute to God nothing but what is warranted by natural reason must either use such negative attributes as *infinite, eternal, incomprehensible,* or superlatives, as *most high, most great,* and the like, or indefinite, as *good, just, holy, creator*' (*L* 31.28; cf. *OL* 3: Appendix 3.6). Humans do not have genuine ideas of the negative attributes, and the superlatives and indefinite epithets are applied laudatively.

Religion, Superstition and True Religion

Hobbes defined religion as 'fear of power invisible, feigned by the mind or imagined from tales publicly allowed'. This is a fairly good definition, at least as regards the phrase 'fear of power invisible'. It seems to denote the genus or general category to which religion belongs. When this first part of his definition was criticized, Hobbes replied by citing a passage from the Psalms: 'the beginning of wisdom is fear of the Lord.' The rest of Hobbes's definition, which seems to relate to the two species of religion – namely, superstition and true religion – introduces one odd and one controversial feature of his definitions.[6] The oddity is that instead of using the phrase 'feigned by the mind' to provide a non-controversial definition of 'superstition' as fear of invisible powers invented by the mind, he uses its negation to help define 'true religion'. It is not the resulting definition of 'true religion' that is odd (namely, fear of invisible powers that are not invented by the mind) but the procedure of using what appears to be the negation of a specific difference (*L* 6.36). This odd procedure does yield an odd definition of 'superstition'. Hobbes uses the negation of the phrase, 'imagined from tales publicly allowed' to construct the definition of superstition as fear of invisible powers not approved of by government authorities. According to this definition, Christianity under the Emperor Nero was superstitious, as were all Protestant religions in Spain during the seventeenth century. Also, neither Roman Catholicism in Spain nor Islam under Turkish rule were superstitious, since they were state religions. This defect in Hobbes's definitions was noticed almost immediately by his contemporaries, notably Bishop Bramhall (*EW* 4: 325). Hobbes defends himself by citing the place in *De Cive* where he said that superstition was fear without right reason (*EW* 4:289, 292). He also emphasizes his abhorrence of superstition and atheism: 'I deny that there is any reason either in the atheist or in the superstitious' (*EW* 4:293). But the defence commits the fallacy of *ignoratio elenchi*; it is not the definition in *De Cive* that is objectionable, but the one in *Leviathan*.

A purely logical and dispassionate objection to Hobbes's definitions of religion, superstition and true religion can be put as follows. Every proper distinction should have terms that are mutually exclusive and exhaustive. But Hobbes's distinction between superstition and true religion satisfies neither condition. The terms are not mutually exclusive, because on the Stuart assumption that Christianity is the true religion it was also a superstition in pagan Rome, as pointed out above. The terms are not exhaustive, because polytheism is not a true religion and was not a superstition in pagan Rome.

Accounting for Hobbes's definition of 'superstition' is a matter for speculation. The 'subversive interpretation' (which is the dominant one) is that Hobbes was irreligious and intended his definitions to contribute to the subversion of religion, or at the very least to tweak the religious. (It is hard for me to understand how a philosopher could expect to undermine anything in the long run by consciously proferring defective definitions.) An alternative but less accepted interpretation is that Hobbes was cynically describing how the word 'superstition' is used rather than defining its cognitive meaning. Hobbes indicates something like this when he says 'men give different names to one and the same thing from the difference of their own passions' (*L* 11.19). Here is his example: 'they that approve a private opinion, call it "opinion"; but they that mislike it, "heresy"' (*L* 11.19). Hobbes's own opinion is that heresy, strictly and etymologically, is simply a personal opinion.[7] There are other passages in which he similarly contrasts usage with meaning: 'For one man calls *wisdom*, what another calls *fear*; and one *cruelty*, what another *justice* ... and one *gravity*, what another *stupidity*' (*L* 4.24). In another place, he explains the meaning of 'the vulgar' as everyone other than oneself (*L* 2.24). And describing the impudent demand of Parliament that the king reveal the names of his counsellors, Hobbes wrote, 'to the end they might receive *condign punishment*; which was the word they used instead of *cruelty*' (*B*, p. 87; *L* 13.2). Hobbes's point may be illustrated further by repeating an old joke: 'You are stubborn, but I am resolute. You are a spendthrift, but I am frugal. You are rash, but I am brave,' and so on. Hobbes might add: 'I believe in the true religion, but you are superstitious.' The technical name for the underlying rhetorical figure here is 'paradiastole'. Quentin Skinner thinks that Hobbes has this figure explicitly in mind, and is concerned about its sceptical implications for moral philosophy. That is, how does one settle issues about whether someone is rash or brave?[8] But Hobbes never uses the word, and what he says about language is easily interpretable without appealing to any theory about paradiastole.

The non-religious interpretation looks for support from other parts of Hobbes's *Leviathan*. Although the chapter 'Of Religion' is often used for this purpose, a close reading of it suggests the opposite. Hobbes says that there are three components of the source ('seed') of religion. First, all men are curious about the causes of things; this feature is open to perversion because people are particularly interested in the causes of the good and bad things that happen to them. Second, people believe that anything with a beginning has a cause; this feature is perverted when people think that that event had to occur exactly when it did, not earlier or later. Third, people tend to remember causal relations; this tendency is perverted when people invent a cause for an event of which they do not really know the cause (*L* 12.1–4; cf. *L* 12.11).

Notice that each of the components of religion has two aspects, an aspect of human nature that does not necessarily lead to a distorted view of reality, and an aspect that does. Furthermore, Hobbes explains how the unperverted aspect yields either knowledge or true belief about reality. At one point he contrasts the consequence of holding on to the unperverted aspect with that of its perversion. He says 'But the acknowledging of one God eternal, infinite, and omnipotent may be more easily derived from the desire men have to know the causes of natural bodies and their several virtues and operations, than from the fear of what was to befall them in time to come.' Then later he says that the seed of religion is sometimes 'nourished by God's commandment and direction', as it was in the religion of '*Abraham, Moses,* and our *Blessed Saviour*' (*L* 12.6, 12.12).

Proponents of the non-religious interpretation of Hobbes would deny that Hobbes means what he says. Instead, he is supposed to be throwing a sop to the religious. On this interpretation, the irreligious are smart enough to know that Hobbes does not mean what he says, and the religious are stupid enough to think that he does.[9] What this interpretation does not explain, it seems to me, is why so many of Hobbes's religious contemporaries thought that Hobbes did not mean what he said, and so many of his friends, whose intelligence and religion are not in question, thought that he did.

Later, in the chapter 'Of Religion', Hobbes describes religious practices of pagan, Roman Catholic and Islamic religions that strike him as patently absurd (*L* 12.13–21). It should not be surprising that these religions would be the targets of Hobbes's scorn. Near the end of *Leviathan*, Hobbes develops a rhetorically powerful comparison of Roman Catholicism with the kingdom of the fairies, that is, 'to the old wives' fables in England concerning ghosts and spirits and the feats they play in the night'. The fairies speak a language that no one can understand, as do the Roman Catholics (Latin); the fairies have one king no matter what land they live in, as do the Catholics (the Pope); the fairies are ghostly and spiritual, as are the Catholics; the fairies have enchanted castles, as do the Catholics (cathedrals). The fairies cannot be captured, and Catholic priests seek immunity from secular prosecution. His unkindest cut is this: 'The fairies marry not; but there be amongst them *incubi*, that have copulation with flesh and blood. The priests also marry not.' Of the papacy itself, Hobbes's view is that it is nothing other than 'the *ghost* of the deceased Roman Empire, sitting crowned upon the grave thereof: For so did the papacy start up on a sudden out of the ruins of that heathen power' (*L* 47.21–30).

According to the subversive interpretation, it is obvious that this description applies to all religions and that Hobbes knows it. However, the religious interpretation maintains that Hobbes is merely articulating the attitude of Protestant religion in general and the reformed Church of England in particular. The Church of England maintained that it had excised all of the superstitious and pagan practices of the Roman Catholic Church.

Proofs for the Existence of God

Hobbes presents several proofs for the existence of God, one of which occurs as an illustration of how the seed of religion can lead to belief in God. Each presentation is perfunctory. This may be interpreted either as a symptom of his disbelief or as an indication that he did not think it needed much proof, because there were few if any intellectual atheists known to him in seventeenth-century England. Sometimes he conflates a version of the proof from motion with that of a proof from causation. He may be excused this conflation since he thinks that motion is the only proper sort of causation. His proof of God as the first mover is typical. A person who sees something happen, 'should reason to the next and immediate cause', and from that cause to the immediately preceding one, 'and plunge himself profoundly in the pursuit of causes'. By this process, one must eventually conclude that there is 'one First Mover, that is, a First and an Eternal cause of all things; which is that which men mean by the name of God' (*L* 12.6).

Although Hobbes uses it to explain the emotional basis for natural piety, he alludes to the argument from design in *De Homine*: 'For men, whose power is small, when they saw those enormous works, heaven and earth, the visible universe, the motion and intellect of animals of most subtle devising, and the most ingenious fashioning of the organs' thought that God was the cause of all good things when he was 'gracious' and all bad things when He was angry (*OL* 2:106–7).[10]

In his commentary on Thomas White's *De Mundo*, Hobbes says that there cannot be a 'demonstration' of the existence of God. This may be because of Hobbes's technical sense of 'demonstration'; if so, it does not affect the general point that he thought that there were proofs of God's existence (*AW*, pp. 305–7) (see chapter 4, 'Demonstration'). An alternative interpretation is that Hobbes was experimenting with a fideistic view about God or was sceptical about His existence.[11]

Faith

The high point of optimism regarding the prospects of a happy marriage between faith and reason is in the late eleventh century, when Anselm of Canterbury maintained that every Christian doctrine could be proved by reason. The divorce occurred in the nineteenth century, when Søren Kierkegaard said that faith and reason have nothing to do with each other: if something can be proved, it cannot be a matter of faith, and could not have any value if it were. Faith requires a blind leap to a commitment. The story of the break-up is complex but, to a large extent, modern science broke up the marriage. It first represented itself as a friend to both; but eventually it pushed faith aside and then developed a deep relationship with it. For our purposes, it is enough to say that Hobbes contributed to alienating the affection of reason from faith, while purporting not to do so. Hobbes maintained that in committing to religion:

> we are not to renounce our sense and experience, nor (that which is the undoubted word of God) our natural reason. For they are the talents which he has put into our hands to negotiate, till the coming of our blessed Saviour [cf. Matthew 25:14–30] … For though there be many things in God's word above reason; that is to say, which cannot by natural reason be either demonstrated or confuted; yet there is nothing contrary to it; but when it seems so, the fault is either in our unskillful interpretation or erroneous ratiocination. (*L* 32.2)

This was a view that he shared with the great Protestant apologist, William Chillingworth. The compatibility of faith and reason was a standard theme among Christian theologians. Even Thomas Aquinas had distinguished between those propositions of Christianity that could be proved and those that at least could not be proved to be false, but he thought that the class of provable propositions was larger than Hobbes did. This was one reason why Hobbes thought that people should not challenge their faith by putting it to the test of reason. Alluding to 2 Corinthians 10:5, Hobbes counsels people not 'to labour in sifting out a philosophical truth by logic of such mysteries as are not comprehensible, nor fall under any rule of natural science' (*L* 32.3). For him, there are some truths of the Christian faith that are above reason, but none that is against reason.

Hobbes thought that God was not an object of science, and that the Bible was not a scientific treatise. When he argued that demons do not exist and that the talk about demons in the Bible should be understood in some non-literal way, he anticipated the objection that Jesus believed in demons. Hobbes replied that Jesus was not instructing people about natural science (*L* 8.26). He may have been echoing Galileo's remark that the Bible does not teach how the heavens go, but how to go to Heaven.

A clarification is appropriate at this point. The word 'faith' is ambiguous. In one sense, the one that has been discussed up to this point, 'faith' means the same as 'proposition expressing the content of a religion'. The Christian creeds, the Shema ('Hear you, Israel, Yahweh our God, Yahweh is one') and the Islamic creed ('There is no God but Allah and Muhammad is His prophet') are examples of faith in this sense. As we have already seen, Hobbes's position is that no true proposition of religion can contradict any true proposition of science. And, because there are very few true propositions about God that humans can justifiably assert, the possibility of contradiction is greatly minimized. Most religious language is not the language of science but of worship. The point of it is not to describe God but to praise and honour Him. In this sense, faith according to Hobbes contains two components: a person and a proposition. One believes the proposition because one has trust in the person who has spoken it. So faith is grounded in trust, and trust is a relation between persons. One can trust only a person that one is acquainted with. Abraham, Isaac, Jacob, Moses and certain other prophets had trust in God because God spoke directly to them, just as the Apostles had trust in Jesus. After his Ascension, no additional people could have faith in Jesus. Christians then do not have faith in God, but in those people whom they trust and from whom they receive their education, namely, their pastors and those that 'God speaketh to, in these days supernaturally' (*L* 43.6; cf. *OL* 3:437). Since most of those who claim to be prophets are frauds, people ought to believe only those of whom the supreme pastor approves. On Hobbes's view, the supreme pastor is the sovereign.

The political point of this treatment of faith is to forestall prophets from undermining the established government. The strategy of a rebellious prophet is to argue that, since God has spoken to him, people should obey him and not the sovereign; and if they do not obey him, then they are doubting God Himself. Hobbes's acute observation is that people who do not accept the word of the prophet are not denying God, but only the prophet: 'if Livy say the gods made once a cow speak and we believe it not, we distrust not God, but Livy' (*L* 7.7).

In another sense, 'faith' does not relate to what is cognitive at all. To be faithful is to be obedient. Faith does not require that people change the beliefs that they have acquired through experience or reasoning; rather, it requires the 'submission ... of the will to obedience, where obedience is due' (*L* 32.4). (Hobbes is alluding to a passage in Luther's *Babylonian Captivity of the Church.*) In short, a person ought to say what the sovereign commands him to say in matters of religion, even if the person is 'incapable of any notion at all from the words spoken' (*L* 32.4). When a subject utters the religious words that the sovereign commands, he is not himself professing what those words mean, according to Hobbes, unless the person believes it himself. Rather, the subject is mouthing the words, which properly belong to the sovereign. According to Hobbes, the sovereign himself is the author of the religious words that he prescribes to be uttered; the subject is merely the actor. This is one of many occasions on which Hobbes adjusts who the author is and who the actor is in order to get the result he wants. By his theory of alienation, he can explain why the prophet Elisha permitted Naaman to go through the motions of worshipping the idol Rimmon. In obeying his sovereign, it is not Naaman who is worshipping Rimmon, but his sovereign. But a very different result is obtained if his theory of authorization is used. By that theory, the subjects are the authors of everything that the sovereign does; and the sovereign is merely an actor. That is why Hobbes maintains that a person executed by his sovereign has technically committed suicide. Applied to the case of worship, the theory of alienation has the consequence that the subjects are the authors of the sovereign's command to worship idols. So, it is not the sovereign who is a heathen but each subject.

The Problem of Evil

The easiest way to become an atheist, it seems to me, is to think hard about the problem of evil. Traditionally, the Judaeo-Christian God has been supposed to be omnipotent, omniscient and omnibenevolent. Yet innocent people suffer; and rewards and punishments seem to be meted out to people disproportionately to their goodness and badness. It appears that the world would not be like this if there were a being that had the benevolence to want to make it better, the intelligence to figure out how to do it, and the power to do it. Hobbes was not disturbed by the apparent discrepancy between the alleged properties of God and the obvious condition of the world. He said that the problem of evil looks more serious than it is, because most people overestimate both their own sufferings and their own goodness (*AW*, p. 460). He thinks that God made the laws of nature such that for the most part the good prosper and the bad suffer during their life on earth in just the proportions one should expect.

Although Hobbes's jaundiced observation may be true, it does not solve the problem, because if there is even one good person – say, Job – who suffers disproportionately, the philosophical problem remains the same. Hobbes's solution is to maintain that God's treatment of Job is not unjust because God is above justice and injustice. Recall that to be unjust is to break a covenant. Since God cannot be a contracting party to a covenant, he cannot break one. Furthermore, if injustice is thought of as breaking a law, God cannot be unjust because, as sovereign of the world, he makes all laws and consequently cannot be subject to any; thus He cannot break them. So God cannot be unjust.

Philosophy of Religion

Hobbes's greatness as a philosopher of religion rests most firmly on his analyses of the concepts of revelation, prophets and miracles. They also in large part explain his reputation as, if not an atheist, then a non-Christian. His critique of these concepts suggests that revealed religion is impossible; thus, the argument goes, even if he had been a deist, he was not a theist.[12] What Hobbes says is that God has revealed Himself to human beings, but that no one can know when or to whom; that there have been prophets, but one could not know who was a true prophet until it is too late for the prophesies to be helpful; and that although miracles once occurred, they no longer do (*EW* 4:236). (Implicit in Hobbes's stated view is a contrast between what is and what humans are able to know. This issue was initially raised in connection with the limited knowledge that human beings have of God. In the Middle Ages, philosophers were rather sanguine about the way the world is because they were confident that they could know it. Ironically, the rise of modern science and its concomitant growth of knowledge has also contributed to scepticism about what can be known.)

The alternative interpretation of Hobbes's views maintains that what he says is compatible with his being a theist. One version of this interpretation argues that Hobbes had both scientific and political projects. He wanted to insulate the concepts of revelation, prophets and miracles from modern science, which aspires to explain everything in terms of causes within the world. For example, by making miracles compatible with natural laws he was able to accommodate them to science. Also, since some political radicals during the 1630s and early 1640s were justifying revolution on the grounds that they were prophets and had private revelations, Hobbes's position is a way of undermining their claims.

Revelation

There are two kinds of revelation: mediate and immediate. Mediate revelation occurs when there is one or more intervening persons or things between God and the person receiving the revelation. Latter-day believers depend upon mediate revelation, because their belief is grounded either in the Bible, which was written by someone who claimed to have an immediate revelation from God, or from some priest, minister, rabbi or mullah, who himself depends upon the testimony of someone else. While affirming that the Christian religion depends upon a true, mediated revelation, Hobbes denies that anyone can know that the Christian religion is true. If it were knowledge, then it would be science, not religious faith.

Since the immediate source of mediate revelation is some human being (such as a priest) or artefact (such as the Bible) and not God, a person who does not believe the message of the alleged revelation is not doubting God but only a human being: 'For if I should not believe all that is written by Historians, of the glorious acts of *Alexander* or *Caesar*, I do not think the ghost of *Alexander* or *Caesar* had any just cause to be offended; or any body else but the historian ... So that it is evident that whatsoever we believe upon no other reason than what is drawn from authority of men only, and their writings; whether they be sent from God or not is faith in men only' (*L* 7.7).

Let's now consider immediate revelation. If a person were receiving an immediate revelation and did not believe the message, then he would be doubting God. But the person has no way of knowing that the message he is receiving actually comes from God and not from some unexplained natural event or his own disturbed psychology. Scrooge was right. How could he be sure that the apparitions he perceived were not the result of something he ate? The narrator of *A Christmas Carol* says the apparitions were genuine. But the story is fiction. The Bible may say that God appeared to various human beings, but what was the quality of that appearance (*L* 36.10)? They were visions, apparitions and dreams. Do they constitute credible evidence? No. They could not have been the sort of representations that would move a rational mind, for God is imperceptible to humans: 'To say God spake or appeared as he is in his own nature is to deny his infiniteness, invisibility, incomprehensibility' (*L* 36.13). The conclusion is that 'in what manner God spake to those Sovereign prophets of the Old Testament … is not intelligible' (*L* 36.14).

One possibility to explore is that there is nothing logically impossible about God appearing to a human being and no reason to doubt the veracity of the biblical author. The weak point in this is the first condition. Since God is invisible, there is no way that Moses could have literally seen him. Also, since God does not have a human body (*a fortiori* not an animal body), he does not have a mouth and could not have literally spoken to Moses. So, when the Bible says that God appeared face to face to Moses, the words cannot be taken literally. So human beings do not know how God reveals himself to humans. When the prophets say that God speaks or sees or hears, their words must be interpreted 'not (as usually) to signify God's nature, but to signify our intention to honour him'. The reason is that speaking, seeing and hearing 'are Honourable Attributes and may be given to God, to declare … His Almighty power'. If God had a human or quasi-human body, then many of his organs would be 'so uncomely, as it would be the greatest contumely in the world to ascribe them to him'. As a consequence, 'we are to interpret Gods speaking to men immediately, for that way (whatsoever it be), by which God makes them understand his will' (*L* 36.9). The Bible often talks about God appearing to people; so it is legitimate to say that God appeared 'by an apparition', but people do not really know what this means, since God is not literally visible (*L* 36.9).

Prophets

There were and are prophets, according to Hobbes. One reason for this apparent liberality is that the word 'prophet' means many different things in the Bible. Sometimes it means a person through whom God speaks to humans; sometimes it means a person who talks to God for humans; and sometimes it means 'one that speaketh incoherently' (*L* 36.7). Also – and this is the genuinely important point – some are true and some are false, and human beings have virtually no way of distinguishing between them until it is too late. Hobbes explains his view by re-telling various biblical stories and by quoting God, or at least Jeremiah's report of what God said: '*The Prophets' prophesy lies in my name. I sent them not, neither have I commanded them, nor spake unto them, they prophesy to you a false Vision, a thing of naught; and the deceive of their heart*' (*L* 32.7, 36.19; quoting Jeremiah 14:14). Although that quotation alone should settle the issue about the reliability of prophets, it is helpful to see some of the problems that result from mistaking a false prophet for a true one. As part of his deliberations about whether or not to go to war, King Ahab consulted his 400 prophets. They were unanimous in recommending that he go to war. Then the king discovered that there was one other prophet, Micaiah, who disagreed. Brought before the king, Micaiah at first lied and said that he agreed with the others. Only under duress did he tell the truth and prophesy doom for the king if he went to battle. In the end, the king went to war and was killed (*L* 32.7; *EW* 4:324, 326). The king took the rational course in following the opinion of the four hundred prophets, but it was the wrong coursc. Micaiah, who initially lied, was in fact the true prophet, but one could only know this after it was too late.

Another story is that of an old prophet who is commanded by God not to eat or drink on his way back from his mission to destroy the altars set up by Jeroboam. He is a true prophet, and he succeeds in God's mission. However, on the way back home, another prophet wants to talk to him. The second prophet lies and tells the first that God had countermanded the earlier instruction to him. The first prophet believes the second, eats and drinks with him, and is killed by a lion as his punishment from God (*L* 32.7, referring to 1 Kings 13). The moral that Hobbes wants his readers to draw from this is that if a true prophet cannot tell when another prophet is being false, how can they? It's a powerful moral.[13]

Given these conceptual problems with knowing who a prophet is, what course should a person follow? Hobbes recommends that people use their reason: 'Every man then was and now is bound to make use of his natural reason to apply to all prophecy those rules which God has given us, to discern the true from the false' (*L* 36.20). Hobbes in effect promotes rationality over faith by making faith conform to reason. This promotion would continue throughout the modern period, conspicuously in the work of John Locke.[14] The end is reached when Søren Kierkegaard tries to save religious faith by detaching it completely from reason.

Granted that the Bible is one's canonical text, reason should look for the two marks of a true prophet that the Old Testament lays down: first, that he or she endorses the doctrine of 'the sovereign prophet'; and second, the performance of miracles (*L* 36.20). Miracles will be discussed shortly. Right now, we need to ask who the sovereign prophet is. According to Hobbes, it is the secular sovereign, the person to whom they transferred their right of governing themselves:

> For when Christian men take not their Christian sovereign for God's prophet, they must either take their own dreams for the prophecy they mean to be governed by and the tumour of their own hearts for the spirit of God, or they must suffer themselves to be led by some strange prince [i.e. the Pope], or by some of their fellow subjects that can bewitch them by slander of the government into rebellion [i.e. the Presbyterians] ... and by this means destroying all laws, both divine and human, reduce all order, government, and society to the first chaos of violence and civil war. (*L* 36.20)

Bad religious doctrine is also bad politics.

In the New Testament, there is only one mark: that the person preaches that Jesus is the Messiah. It is important for people to observe this criterion because St John predicted that many false prophets would arise. Hobbes then infers that everyone should be careful to consider who 'the Sovereign Prophet' is, that is, 'God's Vicegerent on Earth'. Even if

Hobbes is also thinking about essential Christian doctrine, his primary purpose is political (*L* 36.20). He wants Englishmen to obey their sovereign and not listen to the seditious preachings of the Presbyterians.

Hobbes's treatment of prophets sat very badly with Bishop Bramhall. He wrote, 'I do much doubt whether he [Hobbes] do believe in earnest, that there is any such thing as prophecy in the world. He maketh very little difference between a *prophet* and a *madman*, and a *demoniac*' (*EW* 4:324). Hobbes defended himself in several ways. First, he affirmed his belief in prophets and said that he thought that Bramhall himself was one. However, Bramhall was a prophet 'without miracles', one who 'spake in the name of men to God' (*EW* 4:326). Hobbes also appealed to the scholarship of the respectable and apocalyptic Joseph Mede to support his view that there is 'nothing at all in the Scripture that requireth a belief that demoniacs were any other thing than madmen' (*EW* 4:327).

Finally, he refuted the specific arguments that Bramhall raised. One of these is that Christ would be counted a false prophet according to Hobbes's criterion. Hobbes denied it. He said that Jesus was a true prophet in virtue of the kingship of God the Father, who made Jesus 'supreme prophet and judge of all prophets' (*EW* 4:329). He continues: 'I never said that princes can make doctrines or prophesies true or false; but I say every sovereign prince has a right to prohibit the public teaching of them, whether true or false' (*EW* 4:329). Hobbes suspects that Bramhall is not so much concerned with defending the prophetic office of Jesus as in shoring up his own authority. After rhetorically asking who should be the judge of religious doctrines, Hobbes answers, not private people or Presbyterians, obviously: 'Who then? A synod of bishops? Very well. His Lordship being too modest to undertake the whole power, would have been contented with the six-and-twentieth part' (*EW* 4:330). In short, Bramhall's position is completely self-serving.

Another of Bramhall's arguments is related to the one just discussed. He claims that Hobbes's criterion is perniciously relativistic: '[H]e that teacheth transubstantiation in France is a true prophet; he that teacheth it in England a false prophet; he that blasphemeth Christ in Constantinople, a true prophet; he that doth the same in Italy, a false prophet' (*EW* 4:325). Hobbes defends himself by denying the inference. A true prophet is one whose office is supported by genuine miracles. But God would never work miracles for a person who would teach false doctrines (*EW* 4:330).

Miracles

Although the main thrust of Hobbes's view of miracles is clear, there are slightly different accounts of them even within a short space. His explicit definition of them is this: '*A Miracle, is [1] a work of God, [2] (besides his operation by the way of Nature, ordained in the Creation,) [3] done for the making manifest to his elect, (4) the mission of an extraordinary Minister for their salvation*' (*L* 37.7). For easc of exposition, I have inserted numerals into the definition. I will discuss them roughly in reverse order of importance for our purposes.

(4) Miracles are not magician's tricks; they are supposed to have the specifically religious purpose of identifying a prophet. However, this does not hold for every miracle. The rainbow that Noah saw was a miracle, but not done to identify a prophet. Hobbes seemed to be aware of this when he first introduced the topic of miracles (*L* 37.1).

(3) By restricting the intended audience of the miracles to 'the elect', Hobbes indicates his Calvinism.[15] Calvinists typically held that Jesus came to save only the elect, not all humans. (If he had come to save all and succeeded in saving only some, then the effectiveness of the plan of the omnipotent God would be compromised.) Similarly, it was not necessary for anyone other than the elect to recognize God's prophets. In contrast, the non-Calvinist view was that everyone had an equal chance of salvation. Jesus came to save all human beings; those who were not saved were those who sinned through their own free will.

(1) Hobbes is usually intent on attributing all miracles to God, because he does not want humans presuming to have divine power. The exception is that Hobbes sometimes talks about the Egyptian sorcerers as performing miracles. My guess is that he is engaging in the very common phenomenon of truncating phrases for the sake of economy – 'perform miracles' for 'seem to perform miracles' (*L* 32.7, 44.11).

(2) Hobbes's definition implies that there is a normal course of nature and a miraculous course. This does not fit with his general view that the laws of nature (physical as well as moral) are unchanging. It also does not fit his more interesting treatment of miracles, according to which miracles do not violate the laws of nature. On this latter view, a miracle is an 'admirable' work of God, in the sense that it must be 'rare' and inexplicable at the time of its occurrence. ('Admirable' should be associated with its etymological meaning of marvelling at something strange and mysterious (*L* 37.2).) One reason for requiring that miracles be rare is that it immediately undercuts the Roman Catholic claim that every eucharistic consecration is a miraculous transformation of bread and wine into the body and blood of Christ. More important in the present context is the other condition on admirableness. A miracle can be an event that occurs within the natural course of things and according to the laws of nature, as long as the observers do not know what these natural causes are. Hobbes gives the example of Noah's observation of the rainbow. Not only was the event rare because no one had ever before seen one, but it was inexplicable by someone as uneducated in science as Noah (*L* 37.4).[16] On Hobbes's view, both miracles and natural science can be preserved.

However, Hobbes draws certain consequences from his own account of miracles that made him suspect to conventional Christians. First, the more the natural sciences progress, the smaller is the range of phenomena that can be areas of miracles. Centuries ago, a person who fell over dead in the heat of an argument could be interpreted as having been struck down by God; today, it is just another coronary attack. A birth defect could be seen as a sign of divine judgement; today, we look for the genetic defect or the noxious chemical that the parents ingested. Second, to witness a miracle is to admit to being ignorant. Hobbes puts the point more abusively: 'And thence it is, that ignorant and superstitious men make great Wonders of those works, which other men, knowing to proceed from Nature, ... admire not at all: As when Eclipses of the Sun and Moon have been taken for supernatural works, by the common people' (*L* 37.5). Hobbes is clearly counting on the pride and prejudices of his readers to sway them not to be eager to witness, or at least admit to witnessing, a miracle. Many scholars see these consequences as intended to undermine belief in Christianity. A less drastic interpretation is that Hobbes was content to believe in the miracles of the Old and New Testament since they were foundational for Christianity; and to minimize the possibility of post-biblical miracles, in order to preserve the stability of the established government. His view that miracles ended with the death of John the Apostle (*EW* 4:326–7) was a respectable view at the time, as was his down-playing of miracles. In general, Protestants thought of miracles as closely tied to the superstitious beliefs of the Roman Catholics.

What is Necessary for Salvation

According to Hobbes, two things are necessary for salvation. One is '*Obedience to Laws*' (*L* 43.3). The other is to believe that Jesus is the Christ or Messiah. These two elements correspond with the two types of covenant that formed the essence of the covenant theology that was favoured by some early Stuart Calvinists: the covenant of works and the covenant of grace. The covenant of works was the covenant that God made with Adam. The terms of it were that if Adam obeyed God, then he would be happy for eternity. And no other covenant would have been necessary. But Adam disobeyed; and in fact all of Adam's descendants sin. Hobbes's account of human beings is the same. If people had been obedient, then faith would not be necessary (*L* 43.3). Because humans sinned, God made a new and different covenant available to humans, the covenant of grace, according to which salvation would be achieved solely through belief in Jesus.

Unlike covenant theology, which maintains that people are saved either through the covenant of grace or works, Hobbes says that both faith (in Christ) and obedience (to laws) are required. His idea of obedience is like the Kantian good will: all that is needed is the intention to obey God, not the actual fact of obeying Him (*L* 43.4, 43.21). He may hold this view in order to ease those tender consciences that worry about whether the rituals and doctrines of the Roman Catholic Church, or the Presbyterians, or the Church of England or some other church represent the actual command of God. As long as one intends to do what God wants (which includes obeying one's sovereign), it is unimportant what doctrine or what ritual one follows, as far as salvation is concerned. In answer to what God genuinely commands people to do, Hobbes answers: follow the laws of nature (*L* 43.5).

The other thing necessary for salvation is a certain belief, namely, that Jesus is the Christ or Messiah (*L* 43.11). Many people accused Hobbes of watering down Christianity by reducing it to this one proposition. They wanted Christianity to be thicker, more robust and more difficult to understand. Hobbes has various replies: the essential doctrine of Christianity cannot be difficult or complicated; Jesus said that his yoke was easy and his burden light; and the good thief learned enough about Christianity while hanging on the cross to get to Heaven. These are epigrammatic responses. Hobbes also has extended defences of his view based upon theologically insightful readings of the New Testament. As unpopular as Hobbes's statement of the essence of Christianity was in his own time, its content came to be an important and respected view. There was a general drift towards it in the latter part of the seventeenth century, especially with John Locke and among the Latitudinarians. And contemporary biblical critics teach the same thing.[17]

There is also a very different side to Hobbes's view that the essence of Christianity is the proposition that Jesus is the Messiah. Sometimes he says that that one proposition entails all the other propositions of the Nicene Creed. In this case, the proposition no longer sounds simple at all since it would entail the Trinity, Jesus as saviour and many other things.

In any case, Hobbes intended his view to have a political consequence. When there is no conflict between the essence of Christianity and what the sovereign commands, a subject is required as a matter of justice to obey his sovereign. Jesus taught that very doctrine: 'The Scribes and Pharisees sit in Moses' Chair' and 'Render unto Caesar what is Caesar's.' St Paul does the same: 'Servants obey your Masters in all things.' It goes without saying that if obedience to the sovereign would result in eternal death, 'then it were madness to obey it' (*L* 43.2).

Heaven and Hell

Christianity is a salvation religion. The point of believing in Jesus is first of all to be saved from horrible and otherwise inevitable dangers. These dangers are often described as spiritual death or unspeakable, eternal pain. Although they also include a certain amount of misery in this life, the focus is on the consequences to be suffered or enjoyed in some other world and for eternity. Hobbes denies that there is any world other than the physical one. For him, Heaven ('the kingdom of God') will be on earth. Hell will consist of some eternal flames somewhere on earth. At the end of the present epoch of the world, the dead will rise. The elect will enjoy an eternally happy existence on earth. The damned will suffer 'the second death' described by St Paul, by literally being burned by the fires of Hell. Their suffering will be intense but relatively short, since eternal punishment is inconsistent with the infinite mercy of God.

Hobbes's eschatological views have an obvious 'this-worldly' cast. In addition to what has been said up to this point, it should be noticed how thoroughly Hobbes has secularized the Christian doctrine of salvation. The state of nature threatens human life. Individual humans need some entity, not identical with them, to save themselves. This saviour is the civil government. The civil government is a 'mortal god' with quasi-divine properties: its power is irresistible; in effect, it determines what is true or false by settling controversies; goodness becomes identified with the will of the sovereign, and the sovereign determines justice by making and enforcing laws. Ironically, the contemporary welfare state, which protects people from all sorts of ills and promotes their health, wealth and happiness, is consonant with the Hobbesian ideal (*L* 30.1).

Heresy

Virtually all seventeenth-century English and French would have been unhappy with Hobbes's novel interpretations of doctrine. Indeed, part of his reason for returning from France during the winter of 1650–1 was that his attacks on Roman Catholicism in *Leviathan* had angered some priests there (*OL* 1:xvii). Also, English Christians of various denominations were unhappy with all of the elements already discussed and some others yet to be discussed. In the 1657 Bill against atheism and profanity, *Leviathan* was supposed to be one of the books examined. Nothing came of it. Again, in 1666, after the Great Fire of London and the Plague, the search for causes led to some national self-flagellation and the search for atheists. Hobbes, along with the renegade Catholic priest, Thomas White, was again investigated, with no action being taken against them.

For many people, Hobbes was at least a heretic. His defence of himself is characteristic.[18] First, he defined 'heretic' in a way that made the charge relatively trivial. A heretic, he says, leaning on etymology, is any one who holds his own opinion. Probably as a way of tweaking his opponents, for whom

Aristotle was a paradigm of respectability, he points out that Aristotelians were once called heretics. Second, religious heresies are restricted to those named in the Bible or declared by the four earliest church councils; so a new opinion *ipso facto* – Hobbes may be thinking of his own – cannot be heretical. Hobbes argued that even if the charge of heresy were not trivial, either no punishment could be inflicted on him or, at most, he could be excommunicated, which would have the sole consequence that he should be left alone. Very few people in England had been punished for heresy. The most serious persecutions were under the Roman Catholic Queen Mary I, of odious memory. Also, Queen Elizabeth ruled that only Parliament or the Court of High Commission could declare a person or doctrine to be heretical, and the High Commission had been abolished as part of the rebels' campaign against Charles I (*B*, pp. 8–10; *EW* 4:355).

According to a recent interpretation, Hobbes's history is designed to show that heresy has become worse and more common through the ages: 'eventually the multiplication of disputes calls into question the very existence of orthodoxy, and the warring sects argue more and more about authority'. A serious problem for this view, if Hobbes is taken to be a Protestant, is that instead of making the Reformation a reformation, it makes it a further corruption of religion that leads to greater crises. Orthodoxy itself 'unravels of its own accord as heresies and reformation generate more and more controversies about the definitions of orthodoxy'.[19] This is essentially a Hegelian analysis of Hobbes: orthodoxy contains within itself the seeds of its own destruction. This interpretation does not seem to be true to Hobbes, who has a very keen sense of what counts as orthodoxy. Orthodoxy is what the sovereign has declared it to be. In England, it was the teaching of the Bible and that of the first four councils of the church. Orthodoxy contributes to the stability of a government. Hobbes implies that part of the problem in England during the 1640s was the abolition of the court that enforced orthodoxy.

The Church and Erastianism

Hobbes wanted all matters of religion to be decided ultimately by the sovereign. In maintaining this position, he was thoroughly Erastian. Contemporary scholars sometimes imply that being Erastian was tantamount to being atheistic. But it was not. Most members of the Long Parliament and most Presbyterians were Erastians. Erastianism was the official position of England. By the Act of Supremacy, the monarch was declared the head of the Church of England. Hobbes thought that that was a very good thing: there could be no peace if the religious and secular authorities were separate. Sovereignty cannot be limited or shared with any independent authority: 'No man can serve two masters'; 'If a house be divided against itself it cannot stand' (Mark, 3:25); '*Temporal* and *Spiritual* Government, are but two words brought into the world, to make men see double, and mistake their *Lawfull Soveraign*' (*L* 39.5).

The word 'church' has many uses and meanings, albeit related ones. The confusion of these meanings has led to mistaken doctrines, such as that there is one catholic or universal Christian church (*L* 39.5). The Roman Catholics use this false doctrine to press the authority of the Pope against legitimate rulers. Some of the clergy of the Church of England used this meaning to maintain their authoritative independence from the king, even when they supported him and his policies against rivals such as the Presbyterians and Independents. The central meaning of 'church', that is, the sense in which a church can be taken as a unity or 'for one Person' or 'can be said to have power to will, to pronounce, to command, to be obeyed, to make laws, or to do any other action whatsoever' is this (*L* 39.4): 'A company of men professing Christian Religion, united in the person of one Sovereign; at whose command they ought to assemble, and without whose authority they ought not to assemble' (*L* 39.4). Erastianism is written right into this definition, since the existence of a church depends upon the person of the sovereign, who makes the church an entity by giving it a unity that it would not otherwise have. Since a sovereign is absolute, the church cannot have any authority to command, be obeyed or make laws – in short, no authority at all except as authorized by the sovereign. The clause stipulating that Christians ought to assemble at the command of the sovereign was reflected in the practice of the Church of England, in that the bishops, as *ex officio* members of the House of Lords, did assemble whenever Parliament was called into session. Also, whenever Parliament was called, a church convocation was called into session at the same time.

Hobbes's views about the nature of the church have primarily a political function, namely, to ensure that the peace and stability guaranteed by the civil state is not jeopardized by any competing authority: 'And that Governor must be one; or else there must needs follow Faction, and Civil war in the Common-wealth, between the *Church* and *State*; ... between the *Sword of Justice*, and the *Shield of Faith*' (*L* 40.5).

Religious Toleration

Hobbes wrote a substantial amount about heresy during the 1660s, including *A Historical Narration Concerning Heresy*, an appendix on heresy for the Latin version of *Leviathan*, and a significant part of *Behemoth* and *A Dialogue of the Commmon Laws.* Richard Tuck has argued that these works are 'testimony to the terror into which he [Hobbes] was plunged by the events of 1666–8'[20] and that Hobbes was a proponent of religious toleration after the Restoration. There is no doubt that Hobbes wanted to avoid being burnt as a heretic – or as anything else for that matter – and that he greatly preferred to end his days, as he did, dying in bed as a nonagenarian. But it has not been proven that the man who challenged the clerics was living in terror, nor that he was a sincere proponent of toleration.

According to Tuck himself, Hobbes's 'most passionate defense of toleration' occurs in *Leviathan* when he says, 'So we are reduced to the Independency of the Primitive Christians to follow Paul, or Cephas, or Apollos, every man as he liketh best' (*L* 47:20).[21] That it is Hobbes's most passionate defence should be conceded, but it contains no clear passion for Independency at all. The word 'reduced' is ambiguous. As used by some Protestants of the time, the word had a positive connotation: the superstitions of Roman Catholicism have been stripped away. But it could also have a negative connotation. Hobbes could have been indicating that, after a decade of civil war, Christianity survived in a form in which every congregation is for itself. Also, his remark alludes to an incident in which St Paul was criticizing his fellow Christians for their childish divisions: 'for whereas there is among you envying, and strife, and divisions, are ye not carnal and walk as men? For while one saieth, I am of Paul, and another I am of Apollo, are ye not carnal' (1 Corinthians 3:3–4). When Hobbes says that Independency is 'perhaps the best', Tuck wants the reader to emphasize 'best' and ignore the hedge-word 'perhaps'. Also, Hobbes endorses Independency with the stipulation 'if it be without contention'; and at least the previous 150 years of English history had shown that the existence of different Christian denominations involved contention. Hobbes was as enthusiastic about Independency in 1651 as he was about the Commonwealth. He could take it; but he did not have to like it. Without unambigous evidence to the contrary, it is dubious that Hobbes, who argued so strenuously that religion was a principal cause of the English Civil War, who lived through the Thirty Years War and who thought that religious differences caused political conflicts, would come to think that toleration was desirable.[22] Although Hobbes thought that a sovereign should 'tolerate' a person's private beliefs because they were not within a person's control and that it is practically impossible to discover what these beliefs are if a person wants to keep them hidden, I do not see that he was sympathetic to having a sovereign tolerate varying forms of worship. There is no spirit of toleration in his definition of a church: 'A company of men professing Christian religion, united in the person of one sovereign, at whose command they ought to assemble and without whose authority they ought not to assemble' (*L* 39.4).

Tuck's case is also not persuasive, because he ignores the evidence against his interpretation. Only five examples will be mentioned here. One is the illustrated title-page of *Leviathan*, designed by Hobbes, which depicts the sovereign holding a bishop's crosier, a symbol despicable to Independents and Presbyterians alike. The second, mentioned above, is his position that the sovereign provides the unity that makes a church an entity. The third is his insistence in *Behemoth* that religion ought to be law and not disputed. The fourth is that Christian kings are bishops. The fifth is that Hobbes maintained that episcopacy was 'the best government in religion'.[23]

In order to make his interpretation more plausible, Tuck maintains that the sovereign has 'constricted responsibility'; subjects transfer to the sovereign only 'the right to exercise judgement about what will preserve us ... [and] we retain the right to use our own judgement' about certain other matters.[24] Among other things, this interpretation does not fit with the historical circumstances. Hobbes supported the efforts of Charles II to re-establish absolute sovereignty in theory and in practice.

4
Scientific Views

Philosophy and Science

Before the eighteenth century, philosophy and science were identified with each other. Isaac Newton, for example, was a professor of natural philosophy. The gradual separation of philosophy from science began in the seventeenth century. Ironically, Hobbes contributed to it even though he too identified them. For example, contrary to earlier tradition, which took philosophy/science to be any organized body of knowledge, Hobbes wanted philosophy/science to discuss efficient causes only: *Philosophy is the knowledge, acquired through correct reasoning, of effects or phenomena from the conception of their causes or generations, and also of generations which could exist from the knowledge of their effects* (*DCo* 1.2). The only way in which an object can cause something is by motion. Indeed, reality consists only of bodies in motion, where motion is defined as the continuous 'loss of one place and the acquisition of another'. So all motion is what Aristotelians call 'local motion'; there is no such thing as qualitative change.

Hobbes explains his idea using the terminology of Aristotelian physics even though he transmutes the concepts.[1] For him, there are only two kinds of causes, efficient and material causes (and there is no action at a distance). There are two kinds of efficient causes: those that push and those that pull. In pushing motion, the efficient cause is the body that pushes; the material cause is the body pushed. There are no formal or final causes at all; such ideas are not science but myth. Whenever a so-called formal cause is a genuine cause, then it is in actuality an efficient cause. In pulling motion (such as magnetism), the efficient cause is the puller; the material cause is the pullee (*DCo* 6.6, 8.10, 9.7, 9.9, 10.7).

While Galileo was the first to formulate a statement of the law of inertia, Hobbes was a strong and early proponent of it. Whatever is in motion will remain in motion unless something acts on it; and whatever is in rest will remain at rest unless something acts on it (*DCo* 8.19; *L* 2.1). Hobbes also believed in the conservation of matter. There is no generation and corruption in the Aristotelian sense of one unifying form either coming to be or passing away. When a living thing is born or dies or when an inanimate thing is seemingly destroyed, what happens is that the small bodies that compose the thing get rearranged. Such rearrangements cause human beings to have very different perceptions of the bodies, and that is why they think that there are qualitative changes (*DCo* 8.20).

Reason

Science is acquired through correct reasoning. According to Hobbes, reason is computation, and computation is nothing but adding and subtracting. It is plausible that at least a large part of mathematical reasoning is addition and subtraction, or reducible to it. But how can this be extended to all reasoning? Hobbes illustrated his claim with a couple of examples. The idea of a human being is the sum of (the result of adding) the concepts *rational, animate* and *body*. Conversely, subtracting the concept *rational* from the idea of man gives the remainder of *animate body* or animal. (Explaining the validity of syllogisms in terms of addition and subtraction has been worked out by other philosophers (*DCo* 1.2–3).)[2] Even if all reasoning cannot be explicated as addition and subtraction, the idea that reasoning is nothing but computation is the dominant idea in contemporary cognitive science and artificial intelligence. Hobbes's own alleged proof that all reasoning is computation is, however, weak or non-existent; and his position is best taken as heuristic.

Science is not simply reason, but correct or right reason. While Hobbes never denied that there are correct answers to problems, he recognized – as all the great seventeenth-century philosophers did – that people come up with incompatible answers to some problems, and that each purports to have obtained the answer through right reason. The issue then is to figure out some way to settle the resulting disputes. Many thought that an epistemological criterion could be discovered. Descartes settled on the criterion of clear and distinct ideas. Hobbes thought that no such criterion could be devised, because genuine scepticism – that is, the reasonable caution that anyone should have because people do make mistakes – is justified. Reason itself cannot be appealed to when there is a difference of opinion, because the testimony of reason itself is at issue. The solution must lie outside of epistemology altogether. Hobbes maintained that the dispute could be settled only by an appeal to authority; and the only authority within a commonwealth is the sovereign. This is one reason why there is no science in the state of nature (*L* 13.9). In other words, science requires a sovereign authority; it cannot exist except in a civil state.

Hobbes's solution to scepticism is conventionalism. On his view, people must take as 'right reason' whatever the sovereign authority or his deputies – in this case, scientists – say it is.[3] The same conventionalism pervades his views about religion. Superstition is belief in those invisible powers, which is not permitted by the authorities. And, although he defines true religion as that which corresponds to the way things really are, the fact that subjects are required to accept as normative those books, doctrines and rituals specified by the sovereign, shows that he has a basically conventionalistic solution to the post-Reformation worry about determining what the right or true religion is. (I say 'basically' because Hobbes does maintain that Christians are required to believe that Jesus is the Christ, no matter what the sovereign dictates.)

Causes and Effects

Philosophy/science searches out cause–effect relations. Hobbes defines a cause as '*an aggregate of all the accidents both of the agents how many soever they be, and of the patient, put together; which when they are all supposed to be present, it cannot be understood but that the effect is produced at the same instant; and if any one of them be wanting, it cannot be understood but that the effect is not produced*' (*DCo* 6.10). Everything that a cause produces is necessarily produced, according to Hobbes. If it will rain tomorrow, then it is necessary for it to rain tomorrow. If it will not rain tomorrow, then it is necessary that it will not rain. Thus, no event is contingent in the ordinary sense of that word. When people say that an event is contingent, what they mean – whether or not they know it – is that they do not know its cause. In short, Hobbes insists that the metaphysical idea of contingency should be interpreted epistemologically. (Hobbes has a different account of propositions that are called 'contingent'. A contingent proposition is one that is sometimes true and sometimes false (*DCo* 9.3, 9.5, 3.10). See 'Rationalism and Empiricism' below.)

Since philosophy or science looks for the causes of things and all causes generate or produce their effects, scientific propositions ought to contribute to understanding how things are generated: 'The goal of demonstration is the scientific knowledge of causes and the generation of things; and if this scientific knowledge is not in the definitions, it cannot be in the conclusion of the syllogism which is first built up from the definitions; and if it is not found in the first conclusion, it will not be found in any later conclusion' (*DCo* 6.13). If an object has a generation, then it ought to be included in its definition. Hobbes's favoured example is that of a circle. If a figure is generated by keeping one point fixed and a closed line drawn, which is equidistant from that point, then the figure is a circle; otherwise it is not (*DCo* 1.5, 6.13).

Demonstration

When Hobbes talks about demonstration, he is using a technical notion of Aristotelian philosophy: 'a demonstration is a syllogism or series of syllogisms derived from the definitions of names all the way to the final conclusion' (*EL* 1.11.2; *L* 11.25). One consequence of this view is that there can be no demonstration of the existence of God. The reason is that any proof for the existence of something has to include some proposition that is not a definition but asserts an empirical fact. Such proofs can be intellectually respectable without being demonstrations. According to Hobbes, some traditional proofs for the existence of God meet this standard. These proofs belong on the same level as those for the existence of bodies. Even though there is no demonstration that they exist, they must be posited in order to explain the causal origin of ideas. Both God and other bodies must be posited in order to explain motion (*L* 11.25).

Rationalism and Empiricism

It is conventional to divide modern philosophers into rationalists (Descartes, Spinoza, Leibniz) and empiricists (Locke, Berkeley, Hume). Whether Hobbes is a rationalist or an empiricist depends upon how those terms are defined. On the one hand, if a rationalist is a person who believes that all scientific truths are necessary, then Hobbes is a rationalist. However, if an empiricist is a person who believes that all knowledge begins with sensation, then Hobbes is an empiricist (*DCo* 25.1). On the other hand, if a rationalist is a person who believes that some substantive (that is, synthetic or non-analytical) truths are non-empirical, then Hobbes is not a rationalist. And, if an empiricist is a person who believes that all scientific propositions are contingent – that is, not necessarily true – then Hobbes is not an empiricist either. In short, Hobbes maintains that all scientific truths are necessarily true and analytical because they are either definitions or follow from definitions; and that all the descriptive terms of scientific propositions (the 'categorematic' ones) must be correlated with or arise from sensation. Propositions that report sensations or memories are expressly excluded from science on the grounds that they 'are not acquired by reasoning' (*DCo* 1.2; *DC* 17.28).[4]

Hobbes's rationalism in science is especially important when trying to understand his debate with Robert Boyle over the latter's experiments concering the creation of a vacuum by allegedly sucking air out of a glass globe by means of a simple hand-operated pump. While Boyle was an experimental scientist, Hobbes was not. Although Hobbes did not deny that experimentation has its uses, he thought that the experiments themselves played only a small and non-essential role in science. He thought that nature itself provided enough data to set a scientist to work: 'are there not enough [phenomena]... shown by the high heavens and the seas and the broad earth?' (*DP*, p. 351; *OL* 4:241). A good scientist is one who devises the right sort of hypotheses to explain the experiments. In this regard, Hobbes thought that Boyle was greatly deficient. What bothered Hobbes most was that Boyle's group did not use his principles (*DP*, p. 347; *OL* 4:236).

Hobbes was especially concerned about the proper explanation for the dog that quickly died inside the glass globe when the suction was applied. Boyle thought that the dog died from a lack of air. Hobbes demurred. He thought that there was enough air in the globe. Pure or very fine air could get into the globe either through the glass itself or through the collar where the pumping device met the globe. His explanation for the death was that either the dog's respiration was stopped by the suction or that it was 'stifled' by the compression of air, so that its death was more like drowning than asphyxiation (*DP* pp. 354–5, 346; see also pp. 121–2; *OL* 4:245–6, 4:235–6).

The Unity of Science

Although *Leviathan* is Hobbes's single-volume *magnum opus,* at least as strong a case could be made for claiming that his *Elementa Philosophiae* (*The Elements of Philosophy*) is his multi-volume *magnus opus.* It consists of *De Corpore, De Homine* and *De Cive.* Nonetheless, these works have never been published together, except of course in editions of Hobbes's collected works. There are various reasons why this is so. One is that much of the material in them is available in other, often better versions. Another is that they were published out of order and over almost two decades, with other works intervening. *De Cive* (1642, revised and expanded in 1647) covered the state of nature, the civil state and religion. It was logically last but was published first. *De Corpore* (1655) covered language, logic, scientific method, geometry and physics. It was logically first and published second. It duplicated some of the material already presented in *The Elements of Law, Natural and Politic* and in *Leviathan. De Homine* (1658) covered optics and human psychology. It was logically second and published last. It was also the weak link in the trilogy. It added nothing substantial to the doctrine that Hobbes had published in several other places, and its proportions were odd. About half of the book consists of Hobbes's theory of optics, which had been worked out in various versions earlier. It gives the feeling of having been produced in order to fulfil a long overdue promise. Although the other two parts of *Elementa Philosophiae* had been translated before *De Homine* was even published, the latter work has never been translated in its entirety; and chapters 10–15 plus the introductory matter were first published in English translation in 1972.

There are two competing interpretations about how the three sections of Hobbes's system are logically connected.[5] The dominant interpretation is that they are deductively linked. That is, in principle, Hobbes's definitions in *De Corpore* can be used to infer not only all of the results concerning geometry and physics, but also could be used to deduce all of the other propositions of science; in particular, they could be used to deduce the entire psychology of human beings in *De Homine* and all of the propositions about civil government in *De Cive*. The phrase 'in principle' is crucial, of course, because Hobbes did not make such deductions, and – given the complexity of physical phenomena – they could not in fact be made.[6]

This view may seem odd, however, because the deductions necessary to civil governments were given first in *De Cive*; it seems then that the deductions concerning civil states are logically independent of the deductions of the other two sections of Hobbes's philosophy. Furthermore, although *De Homine* followed *De Corpore* chronologically, there is no reason to think that it is deductively tied to the principles of that earlier work, because they do not obviously appear in it. The considerations just mentioned are the basis upon which the second interpretation of Hobbes's philosophical system rests.[7] It asserts that one or more of the sections have a scientific status that does not depend upon its being deductively tied to the others. Its leading proponent, Tom Sorell, thinks that the early publication of *De Cive* proves this. And this is correct. But there is another claim that is often confused with the first and is not correct, namely, that the three sections of Hobbes's philosophy are not supposed by him to be deductively tied. There is a difference between the scientific independence of a particular discipline and its deductive ties to other ones. This difference may be clarified by considering the idea of the unity of science.

That idea, which had a rebirth in the late nineteenth and early twentieth centuries, was that all science in theory forms a seamless whole, because all phenomena form a seamless whole. Furthermore, in principle, all sciences would be reducible to or deducible from physics. This view did not deny the scientific status of sciences such as chemistry, biology and experimental psychology. However, it did maintain that the laws of these higher-level sciences would be deductively connected to the laws of physics through so-called 'bridge principles' that would unite the sciences. These bridge principles were intended to tie laws of physics to laws of other sciences deductively. Instead of bridging principles, it may be the case that the unification would be achieved through definitions that would explain or reduce terms of one science to those of another. Thus, the term 'gas', as used in chemistry, might be defined using such terms as 'atoms' and 'energy'. Although this project of reductive laws or definitions has not been successful, it is the ideal that is relevant here. Hobbes shares the ideal of the unity of science with scientific positivists. He is not saying that the scientific status of *De Cive* depends upon the scientific status of physics or psychology. But he does believe that they are deductively tied to one another, because he believes that everything in the world consists of bodies in motion, and physics gives the laws that govern bodies in motion.[8]

According to Sorell, Hobbes thinks merely that geometry must be learned before physics and not that it is deducible from it. The correctness of this interpretation depends upon the proper understanding of *De Corpore* 6.17. Although Hobbes talks about how 'the person who teaches' proceeds, the thrust of the section is about the proper scientific ordering of propositions, since its title is 'The properties of proof and the order of things to be proven'. The references to teaching then are inessential. Earlier in that chapter, Hobbes says that moral philosophy can be severed from civil philosophy, because '*the causes of the motions of minds are* not only *known by reasoning* but also' from personal experience (*DCo* 6.7, my italics). Far from indicating that moral philosophy is logically detached from civil philosophy, the italicized words presuppose the logical connection. That a science can be taught or learned in ways that do not depend upon propositions that entail them is a fact about teaching and learning, and is irrelevant to the logical relations holding between that science and other ones. For example, many philosophers once thought that arithmetic was deducible from logic, but they never questioned that arithmetic could be taught or learned independently of logic. Since the 'premises of all syllogism [of science] be demonstrated from the first definitions' (*DCo* 6.17), either the premises of civil philosophy are reducible to the terms of the other sciences or the phenomena of civil philosophy are discontinuous with the rest of reality. Now this latter disjunct is false, since civil phenomena are made up of the motions of human beings, which are objects of the other sciences.

The debate over whether Hobbes's political philosophy is deducible from his physics presupposes at least a strong connection between the two. Hobbes emphasized the connection himself (*DCo* 'Epistle Dedicatory'). Leo Strauss thought that in doing so, Hobbes obscured the true sources of his thought. For Strauss, Hobbes had arrived at the outlines of his political philosophy before he became acquainted with modern science; and in any case, politics is incompatible with science because the latter excludes morality on principle.[9] Strauss's interpretation is dubious. The extrapolations from Hobbes's meagre pre-1640s writings to the detailed political theories are highly speculative. Also, since Hobbes's goal was to show that morality and politics could be given a completely naturalistic foundation, his goal was precisely to show how a normative theory fits with modern science.

The Nature of Scientific Propositions

Hobbes, as we have mentioned, is a rationalist in the sense that he maintains that all scientific propositions are necessarily true, and not a rationalist in so far as he maintains that no necessary truth is substantive (synthetic or non-analytic). What is meant by a substantive truth is one that does not merely explain the meaning of a word, but gives information about the world. Rationalists characteristically hold that some truths about reality are non-empirical and informative; for example, 'Every change requires a substance that changes,' 'Every event has a cause' and 'All reality is one'.

Hobbes gives several different impressions of the form that definitions should take. One is quite conventional; his definitions consist of genus and specific difference. Therefore, he would be agreeable to defining a human being as a rational animal. In this example, the definiens can be resolved into more basic terms. The term 'animal' can be defined as a sentient organism; and the term 'organism' in turn can be defined as an animate body. Once one reaches the term 'body', the limit of definition in terms of genus and difference has been reached. However, 'body' itself can be defined as that which fills up space (*DCo* 8.1). This definition is explanatory without resolving the definiendum into a higher category (genus) and a property that divides that category into two types (specific difference).[10] So here is a second (though unnamed) type of definition.

There is still a third type of definition that is peculiar to Hobbes and revealing about his view of science. He sometimes gives definitions that specify how to construct some object. For example, 'If an object is a circle, then it can be constructed by drawing a line around a fixed point.' This proposition does not state a matter of fact about a particular object, but a hypothetical or conditional fact about how any circle can be constructed. As has already been explained, philosophy aims at formulating such constructive, necessary propositions. But Hobbes does not comment on the fact that most of his definitions are not of this character; for example, his definitions of 'man', 'endeavour' and 'point'.

Hobbes's doctrine that all scientific propositions are necessary and analytic is obscured by some of his language. He says that scientific knowledge is (1) hypothetical, and (2) conjectural. Today, people usually think of hypotheses as guesswork and hence not necessarily true. Hobbes would concede that a scientist, working analytically, has to guess which hypothetical proposition ought to be used to deduce a certain conclusion; that does not mean that the hypotheses themselves are not necessary. For example, suppose a scientist were trying to prove that a certain plane figure had 360 internal degrees. The scientist would have a choice among a large number of necessary hypothetical propositions, each of which would entail that the figure had 360 internal degrees. Here are two geometric ones: 'If this figure is a square, then it has 360 internal degrees,' and 'If this is a rectangle (with unequal sides), then it has 360 internal degrees.' The goal of science is to guess at what definitions are the most useful for deducing or explaining the world: 'Nothing further is required in Physics, therefore, than that the motions we suppose or imagine are conceivable, that the necessity of the Phenomenon can be demonstrated from them, and that nothing contradictory can be derived from them.'[11]

Hobbes may well have thought that his theory of scientific method solved the problem of scepticism.[12] All contingent propositions are subject to the kind of doubt that Descartes had brilliantly developed in his *Meditations*. More generally, since the negation of any contingent proposition is possibly true, any contingent proposition is subject to doubt. So, if any propositions are certain, they must be necessary ones. What kind of necessary ones? Descartes has shown that even mathematical propositions, construed as expressing substantive truths about numbers, are subject to doubt. This leaves necessary propositions that are definitions. Although some definitions purport to be descriptive of the actual usage of words and hence possibly incorrect, some definitions are stipulative; that is, they dictate how a word will be used. These cannot be false. In *Tractatus Opticus* Hobbes says, 'every definition is a true and primary proposition because we make it true ourselves by defining it'.[13] In the first chapter of *De Corpore*, Hobbes responds to those who may not like his definitions; he does not argue with them; he simply avers that he is showing what does follow from them. If they are useful, then they are acceptable. In short, stipulative definitions are necessarily true and immune to sceptical doubts.[14]

Truth

Hobbes's views about the nature of scientific propositions – namely, that they are analytic and necessary – is consonant with his conventionalistic theory of the nature of scientific truth. Only propositions are true, and scientific knowledge consists of those that report 'definitions, that is to say, significations received by use and common consent of words' (*DCo* 3.7–8; *DC* 17.28).

One consequence of this conventionalism is that, according to Hobbes, universal propositions that fail to be true are not simply false, but are absurd. The reason is that the negation of a proposition that is necessarily true is a contradiction. For example, given the ordinary meaning of 'triangle', the proposition 'it is not the case that a triangle has three sides' is contradictory (*DCo* 5). The way to determine whether a given proposition is contradictory or not is to resolve all of its terms to its most basic elements:

> we ought then in the first place to find out the definition of both those names, and again of such names as are in the former definition, and so proceed by continual resolution till we come to a simple name, that is, to the most general or most universal name of that kind; and if after all this, the truth or falsity thereof not be evident, we must search it out by philosophy, and ratiocination, beginning from definitions. (*DCo* 5.10)

As Hobbes explains it, determining scientific truth is a purely logico-linguistic matter. One does not look to the world, which consists merely of individual facts; rather, one looks to the meanings of the words of the propositions, which are universal in the only way in which anything is universal.

Language

If one were to ask how scientific definitions can describe or connect to the world, since they are purely definitional, Hobbes could answer that they attach through the objects named by individual words. Following an English nominalistic tradition that goes back to William of Ockham, Hobbes holds that names refer to objects in the world. The name 'lion' refers to and is the name of each lion; the name 'tree' refers to and is the name of each tree. Because 'lion' is a name common to many objects, it is called a common name.

Because 'Leo' is a name proper to only one lion, it is called a proper name. Hobbes does not notice that since he also thinks that some names refer to nothing, such as 'future', 'Pegasus' and even 'nothing', it might be the case that a person would think that a name refers to an object when in fact it refers to nothing. (In addition to referring, names signify. When occurring in a sentence, names signify or are signs, not of things, but of conceptions. When a person hears the word 'lion', he is induced to think that the speaker is thinking of a lion.)

There are two uses of language, according to Hobbes: the more basic use is to serve as 'marks' or reminders of ideas. Having the sound 'lion' helps a person to remember what a lion is. The other use is to communicate ideas to other people. Science depends upon this communicative use of language, because unless a person passes his knowledge on to others, it dies with him (*DCo* 2.2–3; *L* 4.3).[15]

Hobbes does not distinguish carefully between language, on the one hand – that is, the system of sentences that can be used for such varied purposes as communicating, thinking, remembering, musing and so on – and speech, on the other – that is, the use of language to communicate with others.[16] For the most part, Hobbes's remarks are about speech rather than language. He has an inchoate speech act theory, according to which the same sentence can be used to perform different actions, depending upon the status of the speaker and hearer and the speaker's intentions, and the circumstances. The most important example of this in Hobbes's work is his discussion of the use of a sentence such as 'Close the window.' The sentence can be used either as a command or as a piece of advice. According to Hobbes, the confusion between command and counsel contributed to the political unrest in early Stuart England. Only the king had the authority to command; Parliament's role was to counsel him. Mistaking the right to counsel for the authority to command, Parliament rebelled when the king did not follow their counsel.

Analytic and Synthetic Methods

Hobbes thought that there had been very few genuine scientists in history. Euclid had founded geometry; Copernicus had founded astronomy, which was greatly advanced by Kepler; Galileo 'opened to us the gate of natural philosophy universal'; and Hobbes's friend William Harvey had discovered 'the science of *man's body*' (*DCo*, 'Epistle Dedicatory'). (Notice that Descartes is not mentioned.) Hobbes credited himself with the discovery of civil philosophy. The method that Galileo, Harvey and Hobbes followed was that of resolution and composition.[17] To resolve or analyse something was to break it down into its smallest component parts. To compose or synthesize something was to build it up from simpler parts. On the conceptual level, a human being can be analysed as consisting of a rational, animate body; a square can be analysed as consisting of four equal sides with four right angles. These simpler elements are the causes of the complex. These definitions, however, do not give the flavour of Hobbes's view about natural philosophy. A human being, for example, is identical with a rational, animate body; a cause is always different from its effect, and Hobbes wants science to correlate causes with effects.

In the definition of 'philosophy' quoted at the beginning of this chapter, Hobbes alludes to the compositive–resolutive method. When he says that philosophy is knowledge 'of effects or phenomena from the conception of their causes or generations', he is referring to the compositive or synthetic. That is, the scientist begins with propositions that express causes and deduces what effects come from them. To revert to one of Hobbes's favoured examples again: a circle is a figure composed by drawing a line equidistant around a fixed point. A figure composed by drawing a line equidistant around a fixed point contains 360 internal degrees. Therefore a circle contains 360 internal degrees. Hobbes's science is deductive and consists, as we have seen, of necessarily true propositions. At the beginning of *Leviathan*, Hobbes indicates how the synthetic method can be employed in political philosophy:

sovereignty plus magistrates plus courts and execution plus wealth and riches plus equity and laws, plus reason and will, plus the pacts and covenants by which all these things were made possible, constitute civil government. Hobbes's concern with the generation of the body of the civil government is similar to Harvey's concern with the generation of the human body (*L*, 'Introduction').[18]

When Hobbes says that philosophy is knowledge 'of generations [causes] which could exist from the knowledge of their effects', he is referring to the resolutive or analytic method. That is, the scientist begins with an effect of which he does not know the cause. The scientist must then conjecture what proposition or propositions express causes that *could* explain the effect. The word 'could' has to be emphasized, because one can never be certain that the proposed explanation is the correct one. Some scholars have inferred from this position that the causal propositions, being conjectured, are not necessary. But that is a mistake. If a scientist were to begin with the proposition 'All circles contain 360 internal degrees' as expressing some effect and then conjecture that its cause is expressed by the following: 'All circles are figures composed by drawing a line equidistant around a fixed point' and 'All figures composed by drawing a line equidistant around a fixed point contain 360 internal degrees,' then the premises, by the description given, would be conjectures even though they are also necessary propositions. There is a clear difference between the metaphysical (or logical) categories of necessary and contingent propositions and the epistemological categories of the *a priori* and the *a posteriori.* The metaphysical or logical concepts relate to how the world or propositions are; the epistemological concepts relate to how the world or propositions are known or cognized.[19] To designate a proposition as 'conjectural' specifies its epistemological status, not its metaphysical status.

The confusion of the metaphysical and epistemological dimensions of scientific propositions has led some scholars to describe Hobbes as propounding a hypothetico-deductive theory of science. According to such a theory, science consists of deductions of effects from hypotheses, which are contingent truths. The mistake in this interpretation is in thinking that Hobbes means by 'hypothesis' what twentieth-century scientists and philosophers of science mean by it. For Hobbes, a hypothesis is any proposition laid down for the purposes of drawing inferences from it. Such a proposition could theoretically be a contingent one, but as Hobbes actually uses the term, all hypotheses are necessary propositions.

In scholastic logic, categorical propositions, such as 'All humans are mortal', exhibit the canonical or standard form. In contrast, Hobbes thinks that all categorical propositions are paraphrasable as hypothetical propositions and that the hypothetical form is the canonical one. Thus, the categorical proposition just mentioned is paraphrasable as 'If something is a human being, then it is mortal.' One difference between the two forms of propositions is that the hypothetical ones are construed to be asserting a necessary connection between what the antecedent says and what the consequent says, while the categorical ones are not construed as asserting a necessary connection between the subject and the predicate. Thus, 'All crows are black' is true (because it is a matter of fact). But its corresponding conditional 'If something is a crow, then it is black' is not true, because it is not necessarily the case that crows are black (*DCo* 3.11; *L* 46.17). If some change in the diet or environment made all crows white, they would still be crows.

Although the methods of analysis and synthesis are logically independent of each other, they are often used in conjunction, especially with the process of analysis being followed by synthesis. Once an object is analysed into its basic parts, an object may be reconstructed that resembles the original very closely but differs from it in some aspects. The change would be due to the scientist's belief that the original ordinary conception of something could be improved upon. Many of Hobbes's concepts, especially in psychology, should be thought of as rationally reconstructed, and not completely descriptive of ordinary concepts. For example, in contrast with the ordinary conception that the will is free, Hobbes reconstructs will as the last desire a person has before he or she acts. Since every desire is caused, will is caused. A related concept is deliberation. In contrast with the ordinary conception of deliberation as a free inspection of alternative possibilities, Hobbes defines deliberation as the alternation of desires and aversions, hopes and fears, concerning some course of action (*L* 6.49). While this definition does not satisfy the intuitions of non-scientists, it serves the interests of science much better.

Space

Space is 'the phantasm of a thing existing without the mind simply; that is to say, that phantasm, in which we consider no other accident, but only that it appears without us'. Space then is ideal, not real (*DCo* 7.2; 7.3). The reason is that the supposition that space is real has consequences that are unacceptable to Hobbes. If space were real, then it would either be the same as matter – as Descartes held – or it would be nothing. If space were identical with matter, then a vacuum would be logically impossible. Early in his study of physics, Hobbes thought that vacuums did exist but later he argued vigorously against them. Although he thought they were logically possible, he thought that it was not necessary to posit them in order to explain the experiments carried out by Toricelli and Boyle. Every experiment that was interpreted by the friends of vacuum could be explained by the increased pressures and convulsions of the surrounding matter – usually air – which would result from the scientists' manipulations.[20] On the other hand, Hobbes had to hold that space is nothing for the following reason: if space were something, then it would have to be a body (since Hobbes thinks that bodies are the only things that exist); and if it were a body, then nothing could be in space (since it is impossible for two bodies to be in the same place). As an alternative to the view that space is real, Hobbes held that space is imaginary. What is not clear is how it can be true that independently existing bodies exist in space, which is imaginary.

The Analysis of Psychological Terms

All reality consists of bodies and, except perhaps for short times, bodies are always in motion. Given that psychological states and events are real, it follows that they are nothing but bodies in motion. Since these motions are governed by the physical laws of nature, psychology is deducible from physics. Instead of psychology, Hobbes often talks about this part of science as 'moral philosophy'. By it, he does not mean ethics. For Hobbes, the only normative science is civil philosophy, because justice and injustice depend upon the existence of laws, issued and backed by an entity that has overwhelming power to enforce them. In particular, 'good' and 'bad' are not inherently normative terms. The phrase '*x* is good' means 'someone desires *x*' and the phrase '*x* is bad' means 'someone has an aversion to *x*'. 'Good' and 'bad' acquire a normative or ethical force when the sovereign's desires are at issue. His desires are normative, because his subjects have authorized him to do whatever is necessary to protect their lives, and satisfying his desires is crucial to that project.

The basic term of Hobbes's philosophy of physical science is 'endeavour'. That term has its first application to the smallest units of matter. (Hobbes calls the smallest units of matter 'corpuscles' rather than atoms, because 'atom' implies an object that is indivisible and Hobbes believes that matter is infinitely divisible.) Endeavour, he says, is '*motion made in less space and time than can be given*; that is, *less than can be determined or assigned by exposition or number*; that is, *motion made through the length of a point*' (*DCo* 15.2). For Hobbes, units of measurement are conventional, and geometry, as its etymology suggests – 'the measure of the earth' – has physical reality, not ideal objects or abstractions, as its object of study. Thus, if a metre were the smallest unit of spatial measurement, then a motion of less than a metre would be an endeavour. If a metre were the smallest spatial unit, then there would be no 'exposition or number' that could determine the existence of a smaller motion. If a minute were the smallest unit of temporal measurement, then a body that moved from one (measurable) place to another in less than one minute would move instantaneously, according to that system of measurement. Since units of measurement can differ, what counts as an endeavour according to one system will not count as an endeavour according to another. For Hobbes, this is the same as saying that endeavour is 'motion made through the length of a point'. The reason is that Hobbes maintains that points are bodies, and every body has a magnitude. But when something is considered as a point, its magnitude is not taken into account. Even an object as large as the earth can be considered a point; indeed, the earth is a point relative to the line formed by its ellipse (*DCo* 8.12). So points, like units of measure, are conventional entities. Although they, like all geometrical concepts, are usually thought of as abstract, they are not according to Hobbes's rational reconstruction.

That there must be endeavours is obvious, since movement over a large distance can be divided into imperceptibly small movements. Most people ('unstudied men') do not realize this. When people do not see a motion where they are looking, they think that a motion does not exist there. Hobbes thinks that scientists should rely upon their reason more than their senses: 'For let a space be never so little, that which is moved over a greater space, whereof that little one is part, must first be moved over that' (*L* 6.1). Because space is infinitely divisible, endeavours can be infinitely small.

Just as there are endeavours in the inanimate world, there are endeavours in animate bodies. Hobbes is particularly interested in these endeavours in humans: 'These small beginnings of motion, within the body of man, before they appear in walking, speaking, striking, and other visible actions, are commonly called *endeavour*' (*L* 6.1). A current rough alternative for 'endeavouring' is 'trying'. If a person is trying to do something and there is no observable motion, then that person is endeavouring to do it. Think of a person pushing on a stone wall. Even though there may be no visible motion, there are undetectable motions occurring in the person's body. Non-scientists may not have to take account of these motions, but scientists do.

Endeavours move in two directions: towards and away from an object. An endeavour towards an object is an appetite or, more broadly, a desire. An endeavour away from an object is an aversion. Love means the same as desire; the difference between 'desire' and 'love' is one of usage. 'Desire' is usually used when the object is absent and 'love' when the object is present, according to Hobbes. Hate means the same as to have an aversion; the difference between them is analogously one of usage. 'Aversion' is usually used when the object is absent and 'hate' when it is present.

Hobbes is wrong about many of the details of his analyses of psychological concepts; for example, an animal can desire food when it is non-existent and not merely absent. Some of these mistakes can be corrected; some cannot. None of these mistakes should obscure the power of his main point, namely, that it is theoretically possible to begin with a purely material and wholly non-psychological concept such as that of endeavour and to construct very complex psychological concepts out of it. The most basic psychological concepts, according to Hobbes, are desire and aversion, and these are immediately constructed out of endeavours towards and away from an object respectively. 'Good' is the name of the object desired; 'bad' is the name of the object of aversion. Hope is the appetite for something that one thinks one will get. Despair is an appetite for something that one does not think that one will get. Fear is the opinion that one will be hurt by the object to which one has an aversion (*L* 6 *passim*).

So far, we have been constructing psychological concepts, that is, using the synthetic or compositive method. It is informative to look at an example of how psychological concepts are treated using the analytic method (and Hobbes's definitions). Anger is sudden courage. Since courage is aversion to an object that one thinks could hurt oneself but that one also thinks that one can avoid, anger is sudden aversion to an object that one thinks could hurt oneself but that one also thinks that one can avoid. And since aversion is an endeavour away from an object, anger is a sudden endeavour away from an object that one thinks could hurt oneself but that one also thinks that one can avoid (*L* 6.17–18). In its analysed form, the complexity of anger becomes clear.

Hobbes's analyses angered and disgusted most people. He was reducing people to mechanical systems, to machines. They were affronted to be told that love is nothing but desire. And Hobbes never used the concept of soul in his psychology. If Hobbes thought that the word 'soul' had any sense, then it meant some very small body that was crucial to a living being. But the soul was not and could not be an immaterial substance; Hobbes repeatedly said that the phrase 'immaterial substance' was absurd. The idea that humans are machines or dead matter moving around in very complex ways attacked the self-image of seventeenth-century people, as spiritual beings, made in the image and likeness of God. Indeed, Hobbes's mechanistic psychology still offends people, even though it is the working model of all contemporary experimental psychology.

Free Will

The problem of free will is usually considered to be a problem in metaphysics: is the world such that every event has a cause and consequently that the will itself is caused and hence not free? However, the problem is usually associated with religion. If God is the cause of everything, then God causes human beings to will the things that they do. A variation on this line of reasoning is that if God predestines everything, then God determines every event and thus no event is free. The problem also has obvious implications for the issue of moral responsibility. If people's actions are not free, then they cannot be responsible for their behaviour. Since moral responsibility or ethics is closely associated for most people with religion, the connection between the problem of free will and religion is all the stronger.

Hobbes's position, which initially sounds contradictory, is that people are free or act freely in most of the ordinary things that they do, such as walking and talking, but that they do not have free will. One way to see the difference between a person being free (or acting freely) and having free will is to see that the criteria for the two things are different. According to Hobbes, people or their actions are free just in case the immediate cause for it is some motion internal to them. One thought or desire causes another thought or desire; and these thoughts and desires cause a person to act – for example, to go for a walk. Behaviour is not free only when its immediate cause is something external. A person who is knocked over by a strong wind or a car is not acting freely, because the immediate cause of the fall is an external event. The reason why this doctrine of freedom seems unsatisfactory to most people is that every free action, on Hobbes's account, ultimately depends upon some external event. Whatever thought or desire begins the internal chain of events that leads to an action, it is immediately caused by some external event. The thought or desire of eating a piece of cake is caused, say, by the cake that the person sees. It does not seem to be philosophically important whether the external cause is mediately or immediately related to the person's action. For example, a killer is culpable for the death of the victim whether the killer strangles the victim or steps on a lever that pushes a rock that falls on a lever that releases an arrow that pierces the victim's heart, *ceteris paribus.*

Hobbes's denial of free will is a consequence of his determinism, the doctrine that every event has a cause. His determinism is consonant with his commitment to the ideal of modern science, according to which all explanations are mechanistic, that is, given in terms of the shapes, sizes and motions of bodies. Non-material entities and final causes are excluded from being acceptable principles of explanation. Determinism is consistent with Calvinism and the principled, religious belief that God is the cause of everything. So the denial of free will fits into Hobbes's world-view, with or without the religious dimension. However, his *ex professo* accounts of the problem of free will were given within a context in which the moral and religious issues were at the forefront.

In about 1645, Hobbes and John Bramhall engaged in a debate about free will at the request of the then Marquis of Newcastle. Bramhall was an Arminian churchman, and Hobbes, if one takes him at face value, a representative of the older, Calvinistic strain of the Church of England. By definition, an Arminian believed in free will and Calvinists did not.

Hobbes believed that acting freely is compatible with acting of necessity. A person is free just in case the action is caused by an act of will. An event is necessary just in case it is caused. Since acts of will are caused, they are necessary; since human actions are caused by acts of will, people are free. People act according to their will; and they would not act if they did not will; but, from these propositions, it neither follows that people can will something other than what they actually will nor that they can 'will to will': 'I acknowledge this *liberty*, that I *can* do if I *will*; but to say, I can *will* if I *will*, I take to be an absurd speech' (*EW* 4:240).

One of Bramhall's strongest lines of argument is *reductio ad absurdum*: his point in effect is that, on the assumption that Hobbes is right that there is no free will, then laws are unjust, vows are void, there is no genuine choosing of alternatives, there is no ground for judgements of guilt and innocence or the practices of blame and praise; for all of these concepts presuppose free will. Hobbes's response is to deny the last premise (*EW* 4:248, 4:252). He thinks that the widespread belief that free will is a necessary condition for them is the result of confusions that can be corrected through precise definitions and – what comes to virtually the same thing – modern science.

Concerning the objection that choice presupposes free will, Hobbes again denies the presupposition. He says that those who prove that 'there is election' do not thereby disprove that it was done of 'necessity' (*EW* 4:246). By necessity, Hobbes means *'the sum of all things, which being now existent, conduce and concur to the production of that action hereafter, whereof if any one thing now were wanting, the effect could not be produced.* This *concourse* of *causes,* whereof every one is *determined* to be such as it is by a like concourse of *former* causes, may well be called (in respect they were all set and ordered by the eternal causes of all things, God Almighty) the *decree* of God' (EW 4:246).

The Goal of Science

Hobbes's attitude towards the goal of science is wholly pragmatic. The purpose of science is to make human life more comfortable. Truths that are merely difficult and esoteric have no value. The greatness of physics and geometry is measured by their practical benefits: 'of measuring bodies as well as their motion; moving heavy weights; of building; of navigating; of making instruments for every use; of calculating the celestial motions, the appearance of stars and the moments of time; of mapping the face of the earth. How much good is acquired by men from these is more easily understood than said' (*DCo* 1.7.). Echoing Bacon's famous phrase, Hobbes says that knowledge is for the sake of power: *Scientia propter potentiam.*

5

HOBBES'S HISTORY OF ENGLAND, 1630–1660

The Philosophy of History

Hobbes's philosophy is usually thought of as being ahistorical. One reason for this impression is that he represented his views as being scientific and he contrasted science with history. According to him, science deals with what is universal and timeless, while history deals with what is individual and time-bound. Another reason for the neglect of his historical views is that until recently most scholars did not read the second half of *Leviathan* and rarely *Behemoth*. Among historians, J. G. A. Pocock did much to change this situation. He showed that there is a tension in Hobbes's thought between the scientific and the historical, and that the historical could not simply be dismissed. The scientific results of the first half of *Leviathan* do not leave any room for the Christian God as an object of reason, and yet Hobbes believed that God acted in history. Pocock maintains that Hobbes had no alternative but to emphasize eschatology in the second half of *Leviathan*: 'The Christian mystery to him [Hobbes] was the belief that God has spoken in history and had said that he would return in time. The God of prophesy and history was the only God of whom Hobbes would speak; the God of faith was the only God compatible with his political system.'[1]

According to a recent influential interpretation, quite different from Pocock's, Hobbes divides history ('civilization') into three stages. The first is the prophetic age in which 'intellectual cultivation took the form of prophetic arts and divinity science'. Kings were absolute monarchs, unchallenged by priests and prophets. This was a golden age. The second stage is the philosophical one because 'philosophy was secularized and political philosophy was invented by Socrates'. Disputation flourished; it was the time of Ancient Greece and Rome, a silver age. The third is the doctrinal age because 'philosophy has become academic doctrine' and 'everyone has become the owner of a doctrine and a pretender to scientific knowledge'. Furthermore, the doctrinal age contains the seeds of its own destruction. According to this view, Hobbes was in effect a proto-Rousseau or proto-Hegel in so far as he thought that civilization is the source of its own discontents.[2] However, there are several problems with this interpretation. First, Hobbes did not think that a culture's attitude towards religion or philosophy could be used to characterize it. Second, he never thought that Ancient Greece or Rome was superior to Stuart England. And he thought that scientific political philosophy was no older than his own *De Cive.* Third, Hobbes never thought that every person was a 'pretender to scientific knowledge'. He thought that almost everyone was ignorant of or indifferent to scientific thinking, although he was confident that people could be taught what their duties are (*B*, pp. 144, 159; *L* 12).

In his explicit treatment of history, Hobbes uses the property of being theocratic (that is, having God as one's sovereign) as the principle of division. This method yields the following eras: (1) from the fall of Adam until God's covenant with Moses, there was no theocracy; (2) from the covenant with Moses until the kingship of Saul, there was theocracy; (3) from the kingship of Saul until the second coming of Jesus, there is no theocracy; (4) from the second coming of Jesus, there will be theocracy for all eternity.[3] Hobbes sometimes gives the impression that the first sovereign-making covenant involving God began with Abraham. But that is not his considered view. God cannot be a party to a sovereign-making covenant, and Hobbes insists that Abraham is already a sovereign when he covenants with God. The terms are that Abraham commits himself to take God for his family god in exchange for God's promise to give him Canaan. By making this covenant, Abraham commits his family members to taking God as their god. One sign that the covenant was not a sovereign-making one is that it did not involve the giving of any additional laws. The laws of nature remain the only laws of Abraham and his family afterwards as much as before. Hobbes emphasizes that Abraham was the sole interpreter of both secular and religious laws, in order to establish that any sovereign possesses ultimate religious and secular authority and that his 'subjects could not sin in obeying him' (*DC* 16.3–7). In contrast with Abraham's covenant, the one at Mt Sinai was made among the Israelites themselves, who agreed to make God their sovereign. The Decalogue was an essential part of that covenant. Furthermore, Moses represented God in both secular and religious matters.

Ironically, what is most significant about Hobbes's use of theocracy as the principle of historical division is its devaluation of theocracy. Hobbes succeeds both in asserting the conventional wisdom that God has been and will be a covenantal king and in making this kingship irrelevant to the present condition of human beings, since God is not now the covenantal king of any nation. In particular, Englishmen are in the very same condition as the Israelites who abandoned theocracy in order to 'become like the nations' by making Saul their king. Theocratic rule is further marginalized in so far as the role of Jesus and his ministers is that of counsellor, not sovereign, until the end of the world. In other words, the redemption of Jesus Christ has no immediate effect on human beings. It does not initiate a new age in world history. Theologico-politically, there is no difference between the situation of the Israelites during the centuries of the Israelite kingdom and Stuart England. Even the English Civil War, which meant so much to Hobbes personally, is much ado about nothing *sub specie aeternitatis*. In short, Hobbes is able both to affirm the existence of revealed religion and to make it politically irrelevant.

One consequence of the fact that virtually all of human existence has been and will be lived in the era of fragmented non-theocratic rule is that Hobbes has no intrinsic interest in history.[4] Its importance to him, as it was for most of his contemporaries, is purely utilitarian. It is useful for providing object lessons for politicians and political philosophers. The English Civil War is a special concern to Hobbes only because it adversely affected him and those dear to him; and if the right lessons are not learned from it, the same sort of thing may affect him again.[5] As Hobbes said, 'the principal and proper work of history [is] ... to instruct and enable men, by the knowledge of actions past, to bear themselves prudently in the present and providently towards the future' (*PW* xxi; *EW* 8:vi).[6]

Many scholars think that the fact that Hobbes's first major publication was a translation of Thucydides' history proves that he was a historian, or at least interested in history for its own sake.[7] I am not persuaded. A translation of a historical work is not a historical work of the translator. Furthermore, his decision to publish the translation in 1629 was probably influenced by his desire to warn his fellow Englishmen of the dangers of developments such as the Petition of Right, presented to Charles I the year before. What Hobbes cared about was not Periclean Greece but Stuart England.

Hobbes's Histories of the English Civil War

In the mid-1660s, Hobbes was worried that Charles II and his subjects might make mistakes analogous to those made in the 1630s and early 1640s. In particular, he was worried about the overreaching influence of the restored bishops and opposition to Charles's efforts to establish absolute sovereignty. He hoped that a re-telling of the events of the three decades before the Restoration, interlaced with an analysis grounded in his political theory, might keep the ship of state on an even keel

(*B*, p. 39). Although the Cavalier Parliament was royalist, it did not support absolutism for Charles, partly because it conflicted with the bishops' desire to establish their own authority independently of the king's, just as the Presbyterians had tried to do during the 1630s and 1640s. The episcopal form of church government, it was being argued, was *iure divino*, that is, divinely instituted and thereby as independent of the sovereign as it was of the Pope (*B*, pp. 6, 57). Hobbes disagreed with and feared such a view.

The episcopal Church of England took a strongly anti-tolerationist stand, and it threatened Hobbes in a most personal way. After two decades out of power and almost out of existence,[8] that church wanted to impose its ideology and rubric on England. Between 1661 and 1665, their supporters in Parliament passed the so-called Clarendon Code, a set of four laws that were the principal vehicle of their revenge against the Presbyterians and Independents.

The immediate causes of Hobbes's problems with the clerics were plague and fire. In 1665 there was an outbreak of bubonic plague in London, followed the next year by the Great Fire. It was obvious to most people that the judgement of God was pronounced in these two disastrous events. Not so superstitious as to expiate their sins by driving a scapegoat out of the city, some clerics instigated Parliament to consider charges of heresy and atheism against various people, one of whom was Hobbes, and another the Catholic priest Thomas White. Nothing ever came of these charges, nor of others that followed. It is plausible that Hobbes wrote *Behemoth*, which taught that heresy should not be punished by anything more serious than excommunication and that religious interference in civil matters caused the Civil War, in order to shore up his defence. Another possible motive for writing *Behemoth* was theoretical. A history of the Civil War would provide a case study that confirmed the political theory expressed in *The Elements of Law, De Cive* and *Leviathan.* To some extent then, *Behemoth* is an elaborate 'I-told-you-so' (*B*, p. 39).[9]

Hobbes showed the manuscript of *Behemoth* to Charles II with the hope of securing permission to publish it. Charles refused, knowing that the book was inflammatory. He preferred more surreptitious means of promoting his policies. The book was not published until the year of Hobbes's death, when a pirated and inaccurate edition appeared on the Continent.

Structural Causes of the War

Behemoth was one of the first books to give an analysis of the English Civil War. If Hobbes had written it in the second half of the twentieth century, it would count as a revisionist account of the Civil War.[10] First, Hobbes did not think that the war was inevitable before 1640; and it was not the result of either conscious or inexorable forces leading to greater freedom for Englishmen. (However, a long-standing condition that contributed to the Civil War was the seditious doctrine taught in the universities (*B*, pp. 192, 212–13, 233–7).) Indeed, early in *Behemoth* he refers to the stable and happy times of the reign of James I (*B*, p. 2).[11] By Hobbes's lights, the Jacobean reign was truly happy. It was a time of virtually no foreign wars. Domestically, it was a time when the absolute power of the king was taught (by himself and even by some at the universities); and the opposition to that idea could be controlled. The Church of England was episcopal in ecclesiology and Calvinist in theology, just the way James and Hobbes liked it. Even James's failures were right-minded. Hobbes strongly supported the king's efforts to unite England and Scotland into one kingdom: one king, one kingdom (*B*, pp. 33–5; *L* 19.23). If the two kingdoms had united, then the possibility of the two Bishops' Wars would have greatly diminished, as would have the Scottish assistance to the parliamentarians after 1643. Second, Hobbes maintains that the Civil War was the result of the subversive activity of subjects who had pernicious religious views, in particular, the Roman Catholics and even more so the Presbyterians. Third, the war was made possible when Charles gave away powers that were essential to his sovereignty. Fourth, most people were neutral or lukewarm in their political commitments. This was the result of a failure of the government to educate subjects about where their political obligations lay, namely, with the king. 'Only one person has taught the truth about justice and injustice; and that truth has shined, not only in this, but also in foreign countries, to men of good education ... notwithstanding the obscurity of the author,' Hobbes says of himself (*B*, p. 39).

Behemoth consists of four dialogues between two characters named 'A' and 'B'. A, who is supposedly an eyewitness to the events, plays the teacher to B. The structures of the dialogues themselves are not particularly artful. The characters themselves are as nondescript as their names, and both are in fact Hobbes. As Wallis said about another dialogue, it sounds like Thomas talking to Hobbes. Somewhat strangely, it seems to me, A, the voice of experience, expresses the more outrageous attitudes. Shocked, B says at one point that A seems to be recommending that Charles should have collected money from his opponents and then acted 'to fall upon them and destroy them'. A's reply must express Hobbes's mock horror: 'God forbid that so horrible, unchristian, and inhuman a design should ever enter into the King's heart' (*B*, pp. 57–8). There are some sardonic exchanges, but there is no tension or revelation during the discussion. Nonetheless, the prose often sparkles in typical Hobbesian fashion. The opening of the first dialogue is witty and ironic. Hobbes hypothesizes that if times can be divided into those that are high and low, then the decades of the Civil War and Interregnum were the 'highest'. Given Hobbes's sentiments, this seems to be a shocking claim. But then he explains that those decades were the highest times only in the sense that they may have put a person on the top of 'the Devil's Mountain', from which one could look down and see 'all kinds of injustice, and of all kinds of folly, that the world could afford, and how they were produced by their dams [*sic*] hypocrisy and self-conceit, whereof the one is double iniquity, and the other double folly' (*B*, p. 1).[12]

What is most impressive about the first dialogue is the sensitivity that it displays for the complexity of the causes that led to war. Indeed, B indicates that discovering the causes of the war, rather than narrating its events, is the central concern of the dialogues.[13] Although many causes are mentioned, much more importance is attributed to some than to others. Two secular causes may be mentioned initially. A long-standing cause is Charles's inadequate supply of money. He lacked the money because Parliament, using the rhetoric of relieving subjects of burdensome taxes, failed to approve it for him.[14] Hobbes has a cogent point here. Parliament had refused to give Charles the lifetime tonnage and poundage subsidy that it had become standard for new monarchs to receive. Instead, it voted him subsidies for one year and tried to bargain with him for lifetime subsidies. Charles knew that this would compromise his authority, but he lacked the skill or power to get the better of the majority in Parliament. Depriving him of the funds that he needed to conduct his policies, the people had failed to 'confer all their power and strength upon' their sovereign (*L* 17.13, 18.16). The other secular cause, one that triggered the fighting, is Charles's loss of control of the militia and army. For example, Parliament gave itself permission to raise an armed force by the Militia Ordinance, and Charles was twice refused entrance to Hull, which contained a large supply of munitions. The two causes are related in that Charles's lack of money prevented him from keeping an army adequate to enforce his policies (*B*, pp. 27–8, 32, 35, 97–9, 145).

There were also religious causes for the war. There were 'seducers' of various denominations who corrupted the people. In the first place were Presbyterians, self-described ministers of Christ. These 'unlearned divines' preached that each person may judge for himself what is good and evil and has the right to follow his personal conscience (*L* 29.6–8; *B*, p. 21). Hobbes thought that the Civil War could have been avoided if Charles had acted decisively against these seditious clerics. Adopting an act-utilitarian perspective, he suggests that Charles should have peremptorily killed the roughly 1000 trouble-making ministers before they even preached: 'I confess, a great massacre; but the killing of 100,000 [who died in the war] is a greater' (*B*, p. 95; see also p. 58).

The second most dangerous religious group were the Roman Catholics, who professed their allegiance to the Pope even though his authority in England had been abolished by Parliament in the sixteenth century. Yet Hobbes has to admit that they were not an immediate cause of the war (*B*, p. 20).[15] In the third place were various sects, including the Independents, Anabaptists, Fifth-Monarchy Men, Quakers, Adamites and others 'whose names and peculiar doctrines I [says A] do not well remember' (*B*, pp. 2–3, 136). Hobbes does not mention the Church of England as a cause of the Civil War. Opinion is divided over what Hobbes thought of these clergy. Some think that Hobbes is generous in his estimation of Archbishop William Laud, whom he accepts to be 'a very honest man'. Others think that Hobbes is harsh in criticizing Laud for instigating debates over the issue of free will.[16] If Hobbes thinks that the Church of England was a cause of the Civil War, then no significant religious group escapes his condemnation.

Clerics who ran the universities corrupted the best and the brightest of laymen (*B*, p. 23). The study of Ancient Greek and Roman poets and historians corrupted intelligent young men who often went on to serve in Parliament. If they had not been taught seditious doctrines in university, Hobbes suggests, they would not have been so inclined to rebel against the king. Although it has recently been argued that Hobbes should be understood as endorsing the views of Tacitus, in contrast with Cicero, Hobbes never mentions Tacitus after 1620 and has a blanket condemnation of Greek and Roman studies in the universities.[17]

Another cause of the war was that the large cities, especially London, had been corrupted by looking to foreign countries for inspiration about their own policies. Hobbes mentions Londoners admiring the revolt of the United Provinces with admiration.[18] (It is noteworthy that Hobbes condemns rebellion even when it is against a person (Philip II) whom

Hobbes might have doubly hated, once for being Roman Catholic and once for being a Spaniard.) Also, there were people who had squandered their fortunes and thought that the booty of war was the best way to recover wealth. Lastly, the English were ignorant of their political duties: 'not one perhaps of ten thousand knew what right any man had to command him, or what necessity there was of King or Commonwealth, for which he was to part with his money against his will' (*B*, pp. 3–4; *L* 29.13).

The diversity of these stated causes for the Civil War tends to undermine the once very influential Marxist interpretation of Hobbes's motivation. According to its leading proponent, C. B. Macpherson, Hobbes's political philosophy was simply a defence of the bourgeoisie. Macpherson emphasized Hobbes's brief discussion of the contribution made by the London merchants to the Civil War. Some logical problems with this interpretation are that it gives undue weight to certain remarks that Hobbes makes, ignores the greatest part of the text and largely ignores disconfirming evidence (*B*, pp. 25, 72, 126; *L* 22.20).[19]

Events Leading to War

The structural causes of the English Civil War were long-standing, and did not necessitate the war. James had been able to keep the nation from tearing itself apart. Presumably, an equally good successor could have done the same. His son Charles was not up to the task. In the first year of his reign, Parliament refused to grant Charles the customary lifetime grant of revenue from imports and exports. That was Parliament's fault. But Charles accepted the Petition of Right, which compromised his sovereignty. That was his fault (*B*, p. 27). Of 'things that weaken or tend to the dissolution of a commonwealth', the most egregious is being content with less power than is necessary to maintain peace and defence. Once power is seemingly given away, the attempt to regain it is often viewed as an injustice (*L* 29.3). Charles's entire reign was plagued by financial problems. There were two basic problems: (1) he used non-parliamentary methods of raising revenue (Ship Money) and refashioned or resurrected moribund methods (distraint of knighthood and Forced Loans); (2) while Parliament controlled the easiest and most constitutional means of taxation, it never voted him sufficient funds. Briefly commenting on (1), Hobbes predictably claims that the king acted within his rights 'which lawyers found justifiable by the ancient records of the kingdom' (*B*, p. 32).

He is most explicit about (2). Many Englishmen believed that private individuals have an absolute right to their property, while Hobbes maintained that there is no property in the state of nature. Property rights begin with the institution of a civil state, and the sovereign is the ultimate owner of all property. He doles out real property and titles of honour, and he regulates the possession and transfer of all property. Hobbes obviously has in mind the controversies over Forced Loans and Ship Money. In both instances, Englishmen thought that they were unjustly being deprived of their property. Although the king won judicial victories in each case, the tenacious opposition by individual suitors and Parliament itself eroded royal authority.[20] In short, mistaken views about property are a cause of the dissolution of commonwealths.

Hobbes says virtually nothing in *Behemoth* about the first decade of Charles's reign. What Charles's enemies referred to as the 'Eleven Years Tyranny' Hobbes refers to as an 'intermission of Parliaments' (*B*, p. 32; see also p. 66). The decisive action leading to the Civil War, according to Hobbes, was Charles's difficulties with the Scots. In 1637, the Scots rejected the new Prayer Book that Charles wanted them to use. Two unfortunate wars were fought that strained the king's financial resources. For Hobbes, the issue was simple: Parliament refused to grant the king the money that he needed according to his own judgement to protect the kingdom (*B*, pp. 28–9).

The king's sovereignty visibly collapsed in 1641–2. Shortly after the Long Parliament was seated, supporters of the king were imprisoned, and some of his enemies were released. In addition to the impeachment and imprisonment of Laud and the execution of Strafford, Charles accepted the Triennial Act (*B*, p. 73), the Bill against Dissolution, the abolition of the courts of High Commission and Star Chamber, and the Bishops' Exclusion Act (p. 74). Hobbes's acerbic comment is: 'What a great progress made the Parliament towards their ends or at least towards the ends of the most seditious Members of both Houses in so little time!' (p. 74). Hobbes thought that Charles's concessions to Parliament were technically illegal, because they took away his ability to govern, and a sovereign cannot unintentionally destroy his sovereignty (*L* 21.20; *B*, pp. 74, 88, 118). Charles was in a no-win situation because Parliament was determined to have the entire sovereignty for itself (*B*, p. 75).

The writing of rebellion was now on the wall. Referring to Secretary of State Francis Windebank, Lord Chancellor John Finch and possibly himself, Hobbes says that some of the king's supporters 'went beyond sea' (*B*, pp. 36, 85; see also pp. 29–36). It is significant that Archbishop Laud, Henrietta Maria and the Earl of Strafford are all treated sympathetically. Hobbes even implies that Charles acted badly in not saving Strafford (*B*, pp. 60–73; on Henrietta Maria, see also p. 125). He says it was unjust to punish a subject when he gives counsel at the request of his sovereign (*L* 25.5).

While the king was trying to solidify his position in Scotland, the Catholics in Ireland rebelled (p. 79). When the king requested Parliament for money to raise an army to fight the Irish, it refused. It feared that the army might in fact be turned against them. According to Hobbes, Parliament was planning to raise its own army: 'which was as much as to take from the King ... the whole sovereignty' (p. 80). Hobbes thought that Parliament was in the wrong. The sovereign alone has the right to decide how to protect his subjects. In February 1642, Parliament passed the Militia Ordinance that purported to turn over control of the militia to Parliament. Hobbes condemned the Parliament's action as an attempt to usurp the king's sovereignty. The proper function of a sovereign is to protect his people; this requires that he 'be Judge of both the means of peace and defense, and also of the hindrances and disturbances of the same and to do whatever he shall think necessary to be done' (*L* 18.8, 18.9, 18.12, 18.15–16; *B*, pp. 97–8). But Parliament assumed the role of judging the king's actions when they presented and later published the Grand Remonstrance, which catalogued alleged royal abuses (*B*, pp. 81–4).

In June 1642, a few months before the outbreak of fighting, Parliament presented Charles with the Nineteen Propositions. If he had accepted them, his action would have been tantamount to giving up his sovereignty. Hobbes considered the mere passage of those propositions to be an act of rebellion. While Hobbes alludes to some of them in *De Cive*, he explicitly rejects most of them in *Leviathan* and all in *Behemoth*.[21] The first, third and twelfth propositions concerned the alleged authority of Parliament to appoint and remove the king's counsellors and other officials (cf. *L* 18.11, 18.13; *DC* 6.18). The second was that the affairs of the kingdom had to be conducted in Parliament and enacted with their advice and consent (cf. *L* 26). For Hobbes, the role of Parliament was to offer advice to the king, who could accept or reject it as he pleased (cf. *L* 18.13). The fourth and fifth asserted the Parliament's control over the education and marriage of the king's children (cf. *L* 20.8, 25.16). The ninth, fifteenth and sixteenth implied the Parliament's control over the militia and defence (cf. *L* 18.12, 18.15–16). The fourteenth asserted the Parliament's right to veto the king's pardons (cf. *L* 18.14–15, 18.19). The seventeenth implied a right to dictate foreign policy (cf. *L* 18.8; *DC* 6.18).

In *Behemoth*, Hobbes says that the king did not accept the Nineteen Propositions and immediately moves on to other events. He is skirting the fact that the king's response, authored by Lord Falkland, his former host at Great Tew, was a very un-Hobbesian document. It asserted that England was a mixed form of government, not an absolute monarchy. In *Leviathan*, Hobbes had categorically asserted that the doctrine of mixed monarchy was a cause of the dissolution of a commonwealth: 'for powers divided mutually destroy each other' (*L* 29.12, 29.16). The concessions that Charles made to the parliamentarians did not satisfy their lust for power. They wanted 'the whole sovereignty'. There was now no alternative to war.

The War Years

Hobbes has no inherent interest in narrating the twists and turns of the actual fighting between 1642 and 1648: 'I intended only the story of their [Parliament's] injustice, impudence and hypocrisy.' For a narrative of the facts, Hobbes commends to the reader 'Mr. Heath's chronicle', that is, *A Brief Chronicle of the Late Intestine War in the Three Kingdoms of England, Scotland & Ireland … From the Year of Our Lord 1637 to this present year 1663* (London, 1663), the work that he himself relied upon.[22] Even the official beginning of the war, Charles's raising of his standard at Nottingham, is dealt with in passing (*B*, pp. 119–21).

Hobbes does his best to approve of the early manoeuvres of the royalist forces. Although the entrance of the Scots into the war on the side of Parliament was devastating to the king's chances to win the war, Hobbes gives the impression that the war was lost primarily because Parliament had much greater financial resources. The king could rely only upon his own private resources and those of the nobles who supported him. Parliament, in contrast, had control of the Tower of London, stores of munitions, and either forced or was able 'to gull seditious blockheads' into loaning it money (*B*, pp. 33, 110, 112–14; quotation on p. 113).

According to Hobbes, Charles did his best to reach a settlement with Parliament even after the fighting broke out. But after Naseby, there was little he could do but surrender to the Scots. Hobbes says nothing of Charles's double-dealing with the Scots and Parliament. Rather, he describes the various intrigues that involved the Scots, Cromwell, Fairfax, the English army and the Parliament (*B*, pp. 133–8). Concerning the king's escape from Hampton Court, Hobbes accepts the story that Cromwell induced it, but does not accept the more extreme royalist theory that Cromwell intended Charles to go to the Isle of Wight (*B*, p. 143).

Hobbes's views about the status of the king in captivity are contradictory. On the one hand, he holds that the 'Obligation of Subjects to the Sovereign is understood to last as long, and no longer, than the power lasts, by which he is able to protect them'. Since a captured king cannot protect anyone, not even himself, his sovereignty would seem to have terminated. On the other hand, just a few paragraphs later, Hobbes says that a captured monarch 'is not understood to have given away the Right of Sovereignty, and therefore his Subjects are obliged' to obey the monarch's subordinates (*L* 18.21, 18.25). I do not see that Hobbes has a good way out of this problem.

Hobbes's report of the trial and execution of Charles is summary and anticlimactic. It contains no warmth, sentiment or insight. Hobbes does not even take the opportunity to expose the absurdities of a rump Parliament putting a king on trial (*B*, pp. 153–4). His allusions in *Leviathan* to Charles's death have more bite. In one passage, he associates it with the death of Christ, and in another, with the death of Caesar at the hands of many senators, who were nothing more than 'multitude of men' acting illegally, notwithstanding their status (*B*, pp. 120, 154; *L* 3.3, 8.20; see also *L* 15.8). As for the illegality of killing a sovereign, Hobbes says, 'no man that hath Sovereign power can justly be put to death, or otherwise in any manner by his Subjects punished'. His justification rests upon his theory of authorization: 'For seeing every Subject is Author of the actions of his Sovereign; he punisheth another, for the actions committed by himself' (*L* 18.7). In short, the execution of Charles was unjust.

The Interregnum

After Charles was executed, Parliament abolished the monarchy and required adults to swear allegiance to the new government. This requirement caused a moral conflict for many Englishmen. Early in the war many of the king's opponents had taken the Solemn League and Covenant, part of which included the intention to advance 'the honour and happiness of the King's Majesty and his posterity'. In 1650, these same people were required to take the Engagement Oath, by which one swore 'to be true and faithful to the Commonwealth of England, as it is now established, without King or House of Lords' (*B*, p. 164). Hobbes may have been commenting on the inconsistency of taking both of these oaths when he wrote that a person can enter into a covenant only if 'they are not obliged by former Covenant to any thing repugnant hereunto'. His next statement may be a criticism of the Solemn League and Covenant itself: 'And consequently they that have already instituted a commonwealth, being thereby bound by covenant to own the actions and judgements of one, cannot lawfully make a new covenant amongst themselves to be obedient to any other in any thing whatsoever without his permission.' Hobbes then goes on to talk about the injustice of subjects overthrowing their monarch: 'and if they depose him, they take from him that which is his own, and so again it is injustice' (*L* 18.3).[23]

Hobbes was in a morally and theoretically superior position to many of his countrymen in 1650. He had never taken the Solemn League and Covenant, and his theory of sovereignty made it possible for him to take the Engagement Oath, which he did, in good conscience. One of the themes that emerged from the contemporary literature about the oath was the link between obedience and protection: obedience is owed to the one who provides protection. Hobbes conceded 'the mutual relation between Protection and Obedience' in the very last paragraph of *Leviathan* (*L*, 'Conclusion' 17; see also 21.21, 27.24).[24]

The narrative of the Interregnum, which takes up the last quarter of *Behemoth*, is banal, largely a tedious and complicated narrative of various conflicts involving Cromwell, Parliament and the army. The most prominent moral of the story is that rebels are not likely to obey any authority, and they themselves do not know how to govern (*B*, p. 109; see also p. 158). Fortunately, the book ends on a high note. In accord with the seventeenth-century view that revolutions are circular movements that return a state to an earlier better condition, Hobbes saw the English Civil War as part of a revolution 'through two usurpers, father and son, from the late King to this his son. For … it moved from King Charles I. to the Long Parliament; from thence to the Rump; from the Rump to Oliver Cromwell; and then back again from Richard Cromwell to the Rump; thence to the Long Parliament; and thence to King Charles II., where long may it remain' (*B*, p. 204)

Conclusion

There is a seeming paradox concerning the current state of scholarship on the thought of Thomas Hobbes. On the one hand, more people know more about Hobbes's thought than ever before. On the other hand, the interpretations of his thought have never been so various and so unlikely to be settled. We have seen him characterized as a democratic theorist and as an anti-democrat; as a proponent of religious toleration and freedom of conscience and as an enemy of them; as an atheist, theist, agnostic and Christian; and as an Anglican and as an Independent. He has been described as a rationalist in science and, alternatively, as an empiricist. His scientific theories have been judged to have no merit, and to be as plausible as those of his opponents, given the cultural context. He has been judged to be a competent and even talented mathematician, but also to be an incompetent one. In this book, we have considered many of the arguments and surveyed a large part of the literature that argue for these various views. On my interpretation, Hobbes is a democrat with respect to the foundations of political theory and an absolutist with respect to sovereign power; an English Calvinist with a preference for the episcopal Church of England; a scientific rationalist with an empiricist foundation; and a competent mathematician. But I expect almost every reader to disagree with some aspect of this interpretation.

The paradox can be resolved by briefly considering the nature of interpretation. Interpretations are attempts to incorporate beliefs or propositions about some author or text within one's general inventory of beliefs. Parts of this general inventory are connected with the interpretation that one adopts only in the most remote way: for example, Yugoslavia suffered a barbarous civil war in the 1990s; or the earth is more than three billion years old. However, the beliefs or propositions must be connected with each other if a person's cognitive system aims at being a coherent whole. Other parts of the inventory are closely connected with each other in various ways, for example, with psychological laws: if a person wants to get some thing *x* and believes that doing *y* is a way of getting *x*, then that person will do *y*; if a person says something, he usually means it; if a person does something consciously, he usually intends to do that thing. Then there are geographical facts: Great Britain is an island in the North Atlantic; London is located in the south-eastern portion of Great Britain. And there are political facts: England was not a puppet of the French between 1600 and 1660; and no English Parliament met in the 1630s. All of these beliefs are common to educated people.

For Hobbes scholars, there is an additional large set of beliefs that is relevant to most interpretations of his work. They all agree about various events in his life relating to birth, death, education and associations. They agree about a large number of facts about what he wrote and why; they agree about the kind of education that he obtained; his attitude towards scholasticism, how he hoped a large part of his audience would take his works; what he thought about his own achievement in science and politics; what many people, such as Bramhall, Clarendon and Wallis, thought of his work – and this list could be expanded. In short, no matter how much scholars may disagree about certain, undoubtedly important, aspects of his life and philosophy, the disagreements are based upon an enormous set of shared beliefs, and these shared beliefs are much more numerous than in any previous time. However, when scholars debate, they focus on their disagreements and the commonly held beliefs disappear into the background.

One of the benefits of scholarly controversy is that, even when the principal parties do not convince each other of their respective views on the focal issue of dispute, they often uncover additional facts about some more general issue, which then becomes part of the commonly held beliefs. For example, a dispute over the influence of Hobbes's political philosophy in the early 1650s will lead each side to look for books, broadsheets and letters that discuss Hobbes's philosophy either seriously or dismissively. And even if a scholar's conclusion is not accepted by a reader, many other related facts may enter the repertoire of scholarship.

Is the decision about which disputed conclusion to accept arbitrary? No. The best conclusion will be the one that fits most neatly into the large, shared inventory of background beliefs. How does one judge neatness? Briefly, the neatest judgement is that which requires the least alteration to the shared inventory; the one that best fits with the accepted laws of various sciences – physical, psychological and sociological; the one that explains the most about what happened; the one that can be tested in the light of further evidence; and the one that makes the most modest claims for itself.[1]

There is one further aspect of interpretations that guarantees a practical infinity of them. There are innumerable ways of varying certain parts of either the general inventory of beliefs or those that bear immediately on the object of interpretation; and these variations can generate radically different interpretations. To give only one example, what an interpreter will sensibly attribute to a thinker will radically vary depending upon whether he accepts (A) or (B).

(A) 'A philosopher virtually never holds inconsistent beliefs; and, if an incoherence is pointed out to him, then he is certain to recognize it' (as Hobbes himself held (*L* 5.16)).

(B) 'A philosopher almost always holds some inconsistent beliefs; and, sometimes does not even recognize an incoherence when it is pointed out to him, especially when it involves a principle or consequence of his own philosophy' (as I hold).

Notes and References

INTRODUCTION

1. By naturalism, I mean the doctrine that only natural or physical entities exist. By scientism, I mean the belief that the natural sciences are able to explain everything.
2. The history of philosophy focuses on the logical aspects of philosophical arguments; that is, the meaning of and evidence for their premises and the reasoning used to reach a conclusion. The history of ideas focuses on the similarities of the views of various thinkers and their historical connections.

1 THE LIFE OF THOMAS HOBBES

1. We know that Hobbes graduated in 1608 and had five years of schooling at Oxford. That suggests that he arrived in 1603; but there is reason to believe that he went to Oxford at the age of fourteen, which most probably means 1602. The missing year can be accounted for by the fact that an epidemic in Oxford during the spring of 1607 caused the cancellation of the final rituals required for graduation. This could have delayed his graduation by one year.
2. Cf. Richard Tuck, 'Optics and sceptics', in Edmund Leites (ed.), *Conscience and Casuistry in Early Modern Europe* (Cambridge, 1988), pp. 235–63, for the view that Hobbes should be viewed primarily in a continental context.
3. On the sources of Hobbes's life and the best recent biographical information, see the Bibliographical Essay.
4. John Aubrey, *Brief Lives* (Oxford, 1898, 2 volumes) 1:347.

5. The standard view has been that Hobbes and William went to the Continent in 1610 and returned in 1615. We now know that Hobbes and William were in England in early 1611 and served as official mourners for William's father-in-law, Lord Bruce of Kinloss, and William was an MP in the Parliament of 1614. So it has been argued that the tour did not begin until after that Parliament ended (Linda Levy Peck, 'Hobbes on the Grand Tour: Paris, Venice, or London?' *Journal of the History of Ideas*, 57 (1996), pp. 177–82.)
6. Aubrey, *Brief Lives*, 1:361.
7. Scholarly interest in the relation between Hobbes and Thucydides' thought is increasing. See Gabriella Slomp, 'Hobbes, Thucydides and the three greatest things', *History of Political Thought*, 11 (1990), 565–86, and the literature cited there.
8. Aubrey, *Brief Lives* 1:351–2.
9. Aubrey, *Brief Lives* 1:347–9.
10. Aubrey, *Brief Lives* 1:349.
11. Donald Hanson, in 'The meaning of "Demonstration" in Hobbes's science', *History of Political Thought*, 11 (1990), pp. 587–626, attacks this view as anachronistic. According to him, geometry primarily refers to a method of reasoning backwards (analysis) from the problem to a solution.
12. Richard Tuck, 'Hobbes and Descartes', in G. A. J. Rogers and Alan Ryan (eds), *Perspectives on Thomas Hobbes* (Oxford, 1988), pp. 11–41.
13. F. Brandt, *Thomas Hobbes's Mechanical Conception of Nature* (Copenhagen, 1928), pp. 129–42.
14. Aubrey, *Brief Lives* 1:353.
15. David Johnston, *The Rhetoric of Leviathan* (Princeton, 1986), p. xx.
16. Aubrey, *Brief Lives* 1:351.
17. *Six Lessons to the Professors of Mathematics* (*EW* 7:336); see also *Considerations Upon the Reputation, Loyalty, Manners, and Religion of Thomas Hobbes* (*EW* 4:421).
18. Quentin Skinner in 'Conquest and consent: Thomas Hobbes and the Engagement Controversy', in G. E. Aylmer (ed.), *The Interregnum: The Quest for Settlement, 1646–1660* (London, 1972), said that Hobbes supported 'all the most characteristic claims of the *de facto* theorists' (p. 95). He has since retracted this view in 'Thomas Hobbes on the proper signification of liberty', *Transactions of the Royal Historical Society*, 5th series, 40 (1990),

p. 145 n. 155. See also Glenn Burgess, 'Contexts for Hobbes's *Leviathan*', *Political Studies*, 11 (1990), pp. 675–702; Stephen State, 'Text and context', *Historical Journal*, 28 (1985), pp. 27–50; John M. Wallace, *Destiny His Choice* (Cambridge, 1968); Richard Tuck, *Philosophy and Government, 1572–1651* (Cambridge, 1993), pp. 253–9; and A. P. Martinich, *The Two Gods of Leviathan* (New York, 1992), pp. 357–61.

19. Erastianism, named after Thomas Erastus, is the doctrine that the secular government has authority over the church. Erastus was not an Erastian; Augustine was not an Augustinian, Thomas Aquinas was not a Thomist, and Hobbes, I maintain, was not a Hobbist. (The term 'Hobbist' came to be used pejoratively in the late seventeenth century to refer indiscriminately to people who were considered atheistic, irreligious, immoral or politically dangerous.)
20. 'The prose life', tr. Mary Lyons, in Thomas Hobbes, *Human Nature and De Corpore Politico*, ed. J. C. A. Gaskin (Oxford, 1994), pp. 250–1.
21. Kinch Hoekstra has influenced my position here.
22. Aubrey, *Brief Lives* 1:340.
23. Edward Hyde, the Earl of Clarendon, *A Brief View and Survey of the Dangerous and Pernicious Errors to Church and State, In Mr Hobbes's Book Entitled Leviathan* (London, 1676), p. 9.
24. *Historical Manuscripts Commission*, 8th report, pp. 111, 112.
25. Cf. Richard Tuck, 'Hobbes and Locke on toleration', in *Thomas Hobbes and Political Theory*, ed. Mary Dietz (Lawrence, KS, 1990), pp. 157–8; Tuck, *Philosophy and Government, 1572–1651*, pp. 338–9.
26. David Johnston, 'Hobbes's mortalism', *History of Political Thought*, 10 (1989), pp. 647–63, thinks that Hobbes adopted mortalism as a way of strengthening the control of secular authority by reducing the consequences of violating divine sanctions: cf. Martinich, *The Two Gods of Leviathan*, pp. 262–6.
27. See James Axtell, 'The mechanics of opposition', *Bulletin of the Institute of Historical Research*, 38 (1965), 102–11. Tuck in 'Hobbes and Locke on toleration' infers that Hobbes wrote a 'defence of Scargill' from Aubrey's report that Hobbes wrote 'concerning Dr. Scargill's recantation sermon' (Aubrey, *Brief Lives* 1:360).
28. Steven Shapin and Simon Schaffer, *Leviathan and the Air-Pump* (Princeton, 1985).
29. Shapin and Schaffer, *Leviathan and the Air-Pump*, p. 346; see also pp. 121–2.

30. Noel Malcolm, 'Hobbes and the Royal Society', in *Perspectives on Thomas Hobbes* (Oxford, 1988), pp. 43–66.
31. Aubrey, *Brief Lives* 1:344–5.
32. Aubrey, *Brief Lives* 1:346.
33. Allan Pritchard, 'The last days of Hobbes', *Bodleian Library Record*, 10 (1980) 178–87.
34. Quoted from David Wootton (ed.), *Divine Right and Democracy* (Harmondsworth, 1986), pp. 121, 122, 125.
35. Eleonore Stump (ed.), *Reasoned Faith: Essays in Philosophical Theology in Honor of Norman Kretzmann* (Ithaca, NY, 1993).

2 POLITICAL THEORY

1. Richard Tuck argues that the modern tradition begins with Hugo Grotius. Several of his works are essential reading: 'Grotius, Carneades, and Hobbes', in *Grotiana*, new series, 4 (1983), pp. 43–62; 'Optics and sceptics', in Edmund Leites (ed.), *Conscience and Casuistry in Early Modern Europe* (Cambridge, 1988), pp. 235–63; and 'The "modern theory" of natural law', in Anthony Pagden (ed.), *The Languages of Political Theory in Early-Modern Europe* (Cambridge, 1987), pp. 99–119; and *Philosophy and Government 1572–1651* (Cambridge, 1993). Tuck emphasizes the relation between the project of modern political philosophy and the challenge of scepticism.
2. Hobbes blames the universities for failing to fulfil their educational mission (*B*, p. 58 and *passim*). S. A. Lloyd, *Ideals as Interests in Hobbes's Leviathan* (Cambridge, 1992) is very good on this point; see pp. 159–66, 219–21 and 207–12.
3. Gregory Kavka, *Hobbesian Moral and Political Theory* (Princeton, 1986), p. 64.
4. Robert Filmer, *Patriarcha and Other Writings*, ed. Johann P. Sommerville (Cambridge, 1991), p. 188.
5. Jean Hampton, *Hobbes and the Social Contract Tradition* (Cambridge, 1986), pp. 58–89. See also F. S. McNeilly, *The Anatomy of Leviathan* (New York, 1968) and Gregory Kavka, *Hobbesian Moral and Political Theory*, pp. 96–100.
6. To my recollection, the phrases 'primary' and 'secondary state of nature' were coined by Martinich in *The Two Gods of Leviathan*, pp. 76–9.

7. Clarendon, *A Brief View and Survey of the Dangerous and. Pernicious Errors to Church and State in Mr. Hobbes's Book Entitled Leviathan* (1676), p. 181.
8. The numbers one, seven and ten are not significant. All that is required is a relative ordering of benefits in the way described. A good explanation of game theory is Michael D. Resnik, *Choices* (Minneapolis, 1987).
9. The most important applications of game theory to Hobbesian explication are David Gauthier, *The Logic of Leviathan* (Oxford, 1969), Gregory S. Kavka, *Hobbesian Moral and Political Theory*, Jean Hampton, *Thomas Hobbes and the Social Contract Tradition* (Cambridge, 1986) and Jody S. Kraus, *The Limits of Hobbesian Contractarianism* (Cambridge, 1993).
10. Alan Ryan, 'Hobbes and individualism', in *Perspectives on Thomas Hobbes*, p. 92.
11. Hobbes says: 'and some that in all other things have disallowed the violation of Faith; yet have allowed it, when it is for the getting of Kingdom' (*L* 15.4).
12. Leo Strauss thinks that the crucial difference between medieval and modern political theories is that while medieval ones are grounded in a conception of objective natural law, modern ones are grounded in the idea of rights, 'of subjective claims, originating in the human will' (*The Political Philosophy of Hobbes* (Chicago, 1936), pp. vii–viii).
13. J. W. N. Watkins, *Hobbes's System of Ideas*, 2nd edn (London, 1973), pp. 55–68. Watkins's term is Kantian. He puts his thesis in this way because he is specifically controverting the view of A. E. Taylor, who maintained that Hobbes was a kind of proto-Kantian. According to Taylor, Hobbes's laws of nature are 'categorical imperatives' and *eo ipso* moral laws. The general point that Hobbes's laws of nature are genuine laws with a deontological force – that is, they impose obligations on people – was refined by Howard Warrender in *The Political Philosophy of Hobbes* (Oxford, 1957). While Warrender was universally respected, his views were generally rejected; see various articles in K. C. Brown (ed.), *Hobbes Studies* (Oxford, 1965), Gauthier, *The Logic of Leviathan*, pp. 155–7, and Hampton, *Thomas Hobbes and the Social Contract Tradition*, pp. 29–34. A revised version of the Taylor–Warrender thesis has been presented by Martinich, *The Two Gods of Leviathan*.
14. Depending upon whether they wanted Hobbes to be a liberal or supporter of toleration, on the one hand, or a conservative or

Erastian, on the other, his later contemporaries and current scholars emphasize (A) or (B). See Tuck, 'Hobbes and Locke on toleration' and Mark Goldie, 'The reception of Hobbes', in J. H. Burns (ed.), *The Cambridge History of Political Thought, 1450–1700* (Cambridge, 1991), pp. 613–14, for further references.

15. Dudley Digges, an associate of the Tew Circle, who certainly had read Hobbes, thought that subjects gave up all of their rights; see Tuck, *Philosophy and Government*, pp. 274–6.
16. See Hampton, *Hobbes and the Social Contract Tradition*, pp. 114–31 and 256–66. Some scholars conflate authorization and alienation, e.g. Michael Oakeshott, 'Introduction', *Leviathan*, p. ix; see Gauthier, *The Logic of Leviathan*, pp. 153–5, for a criticism.
17. Hampton, *Hobbes and the Social Contract Tradition*, pp. 166–73; Stanley Moore, 'Hobbes on obligation, moral and political', *Journal of the History of Philosophy*, 10 (1972), pp. 29–42.
18. Lloyd has the mistaken impression that Hobbes allows for non-absolute sovereignty (*Ideals as Interests in Hobbes's Leviathan*, pp. 293–4); cf. *EL* 2.1.14, 2.1.19, 2.8.7; and *L* 30.5, 42.82.
19. When Hobbes defines absolute sovereignty as 'power unlimited' he means power unlimited in any dimension (*L* 22.5). In addition, the sovereign also has to have sufficient power to be able to protect subjects from each other and from invaders. Two or three people gathered together typically do not have the critical mass needed for sovereignty.
20. James VI and I, *A Speech to the Lords and Commons of the Parliament at White-Hall*, quoted from David Wootton (ed.), *Divine Right and Democracy* (Harmondsworth, 1986), p. 107.
21. This is similar to Walter Ullmann's distinction between descending and ascending theories (Walter Ullmann, *A History of Political Thought: The Middle Ages*, revised edn (Harmondsworth, 1970), pp. 12–13); also, John Sanderson, *But the People's Creatures: The Philosophical Basis of The English Civil War* (Manchester, 1989), pp. 86–101.
22. Robert Filmer, *Patriarcha and Other Writings*, pp. 184–5. Hobbes's unusual combination of democratic principles with absolutism explains the apt descrition of him, 'radical in the service of reaction': John Tulloch, *Rational Theology and Christian Philosophy in England in the Seventeenth Century* (Edinburgh, 1874).
23. 'The virtue of a subject is comprehended wholly in obedience to the laws of the commonwealth' (*B*, p. 44).
24. Richard Tuck, *Philosophy and Government 1572–1651*: Grotius 'was the most creative figure in this tradition' (p. xv); but 'Hobbes saw deeper' (p. xvii).

25. Quoted from John Marshall, 'John Locke and Latitudinarianism', in *Philosophy, Science, and Religion in England, 1640–1700* (Cambridge, 1992), p. 258.

3 RELIGIOUS VIEWS

1. Aubrey, *Brief Lives* 1:353.
2. The strongest and most sustained case against his possible theism was presented by Edwin Curley, '"I durst not write so boldly" or How to read Hobbes' theological–political treatise', in Daniela Bostrenghi (ed.), *Hobbes e Spinoza* (Napoli, 1992). For other references, see the Bibliographical Essay.
3. For various interpretations, see: Eldon Eisenach, *Two Worlds of Liberalism: Religion and Politics in Hobbes, Locke and Mill* (Chicago, 1981); Johann Sommerville, *Thomas Hobbes: Political Ideas in Historical Context* (New York, 1992); Richard Tuck, *Hobbes* (Oxford, 1989).
4. Ian T. Ramsey, *Religious Language: An Empirical Placing of Theological Phrases* (London, 1957).
5. Thomas Aquinas, *Summa Theologiae* I, q. 3, introduction.
6. Kinch Hoekstra suggests an alternative interpretation, as follows. For Hobbes, religion and superstition are disjoint. Both are fear of invisible powers. Religion comes from tales publicly allowed; superstition comes from those not publicly allowed (*L* 6.36, 27.20; *OL* 3:18.16, Appendix 3.9; *EL* 26.11). Hoekstra thinks that these definitions are supposed to be relativistic in the same way that 'good' and 'evil' are for Hobbes: just as something can be good for Tom and evil for Dick, something can be religion for Tom and superstition for Harry. Hoekstra's interpretation is not consistent with *EW* 4:292, nor – in my opinion – with the whole of Chapter 8 of *Leviathan.* If only true religion were religion, then religion would not be characteristic of human beings. Also, the phrase 'true religion' would be pleonastic and would not have needed to be defined at all.
7. *L* 11.19, 42.130; *B*, p. 8–9; *EW* 4:376, 387, 399; *EW* 6:97, 104, 174.
8. Quentin Skinner argues that Hobbes is exploiting the rhetorical notion of 'paradiastole': see Skinner, 'Thomas Hobbes: Rhetoric and the construction of morality', *Proceedings of the British Academy*, 76 (1991), pp. 1–61; Nicholas Phillipson and Quentin Skinner (eds), *Political Discourse in Early Modern Britain* (Cambridge, 1993), pp. 63–93, and *Reason and Rhetoric in the Philosophy of Hobbes* (Cambridge, 1996).

9. Leo Strauss, *Persecution and the Art of Writing* (Glencoe, IL., 1952), p. 25; David Berman, *A History of Atheism in England: From Hobbes to Russell* (London, 1988), pp. 66–7.
10. The translation of this passage is from Bernard Gert (ed.), *Man and Citizen* (Garden City, NY, 1972), p. 58.
11. Curley, 'I durst not write so boldly', *Hobbes e Spinoza*, pp. 577–84.
12. A theist is a person who believes that there is a God who is concerned with and takes care of the world. A deist is a person who believes that God exists but has no, or very little, concern with or care for the world.
13. For Hobbes's treatment of prophets, see *L* 36.7–20.
14. John Marshall, *John Locke: Resistance, Religion, and Responsibility* (Cambridge, 1994).
15. On the issue of Hobbes's alleged English Calvinism, see E. M. Curley, 'Calvin and Hobbes', *Journal of the History of Philosophy*, 34 (1996) no. 2, A. P. Martinich, 'On the proper interpretation of Hobbes's philosophy', in the same journal and issue, and Curley's reply there. For a survey of what Calvinism meant in Stuart England, see Margo Todd (ed.), *Reformation to Revolution* (London, 1995), pp. 54, 72–3, 179–207.
16. René Descartes is typically credited with discovering the laws of the rainbow. However, some have charged Descartes with plagiarizing some of his material from the ecumenist Marc Antonio De Dominis, whose work Hobbes could well have known about (Noel Malcolm, *De Dominis (1520–1624)*, London, 1984).
17. John Locke, 'The reasonableness of Christianity' (London, 1695) par. 26; John Marshall, *John Locke: Resistance, Religion and Responsibility*, pp. 427–9; John Marshall, 'Locke and Latitudinarianism', in Richard Kroll, Richard Ashcraft, and Perez Zagorin (eds), *Philosophy, Science, and Religion in England*, (Cambridge, 1992), pp. 263–4; Johann Sommerville, *Thomas Hobbes* (London, 1992), pp. 145–8; C. F. D. Moule, *The Birth of the New Testament*, 3rd edn (San Francisco, 1982), pp. 30–2 and *passim*.
18. He has five prominent discussions of it: *Behemoth*, *EW* 6:164, 174–6; *Dialogue … of the Common Laws*, pp. 37, 96–109, 119, 128; 'An historical narration on heresy and the punishment thereof', *EW* 4:385–408; 'Historia ecclesiatica', *OL* 5:341–408, and *Leviathan*, Appendix, 2; *OL* 3. Important discussions of this topic are Richard Tuck, 'Hobbes and Locke on toleration', in *Thomas Hobbes and Political Theory* (Lawrence, KS, 1990), pp. 153–71; and

Robert Kraynak, *History and Modernity in the Thought of Thomas Hobbes* (Ithaca, NY, 1990), pp. 40–4.

19. Kraynak, *History and Modernity*, pp. 43, 42–3.
20. Tuck, 'Hobbes and Locke on toleration', p. 159.
21. Tuck, 'Hobbes and Locke on toleration', p. 163.
22. A number of distinguished scholars have argued that Hobbes favoured religious toleration. See, for example: two essays by Alan Ryan, 'Hobbes, toleration, and the inner life', in David Miller and Lary Siedentrop (eds), *The Nature of Political Theory* (Oxford, 1983), pp. 197–218, and Alan Ryan, 'A more tolerant Hobbes?', in Susan Mendus (ed.), *Essays on Toleration* (Cambridge, 1988); Johann Sommerville, *Thomas Hobbes: Political Ideas in Historical Context* (New York, 1992), pp. 149–56; Richard Tuck, 'Hobbes and Locke on toleration'; Mary Dietz (ed.), *Thomas Hobbes and Political Theory* (Lawrence, KS, 1990), pp. 153–71; and Richard Tuck, *Philosophy and Government, 1572–1651* (Cambridge, 1993), 333–5.
23. *L* 47.20; *B*, pp. 13–14, 46, 90; 'An answer to Bishop Bramhall', EW 4:363; see also p. 354.
24. Tuck, 'Hobbes and Locke on toleration', p. 165.

4 SCIENTIFIC VIEWS

1. Hobbes's transformation of Aristotelian cosmology is an explicit theme of Thomas Spragens's *The Politics of Motion* (Lexington, KY, 1973).
2. Fred Sommers, 'The calculus of terms', *Mind*, 79 (1970), pp. 1–39; Hungerland and George Vick, 'Hobbes's theory of language, speech, and reasoning', in Thomas Hobbes, *Part One of De Corpore*, ed. Aloysius Martinich (New York, 1981), pp. 105–27.
3. The work of Shapin and Schaffer, *Leviathan and the Air Pump*, is relevant here. See also Tuck, *Philosophy and Government, 1572–1651* (Cambridge, 1993), pp. 300–1.
4. Cf. Tom Sorell uses *EL* 6.6 as evidence that Hobbes thinks that science includes empirical, non-definitional propositions (see *Hobbes* (London, 1986) pp. 41–2). But Hobbes says that such propositions are opinions and thus implies that they are not part of science (*EL* 6.1–4).
5. The best of these treatments is in J. W. N. Watkins, *Hobbes's System of Ideas*, 2nd edn (London, 1973). Other notable works

are R. S. Peters, *Hobbes* (Harmondsworth, 1956), p. 87; C. B. Macpherson, *The Political Philosophy of Possessive Individualism* (Oxford, 1962), p. 10; David Gauthier, *The Logic of Leviathan* (Oxford, 1962), p. 3.

6. Cf. Donald W. Hanson, 'The meaning of "demonstration" in Hobbes's science', *History of Political Thought,* 11 (1990), pp. 587–626.
7. Tom Sorell, *Hobbes.*
8. On the idea of the unity of science, see Robert L. Causey, *The Unity of Science* (Dordrecht, 1977).
9. Leo Strauss, *The Political Philosophy of Hobbes* (Chicago, 1952), pp. x–xiii, 5–7; cf. Watkins, *Hobbes's System of Ideas,* pp. 14–17.
10. On genus and difference, see *DCo* 6.14.
11. *Tractatus Opticus*; quoted from Richard Tuck, 'Optics and sceptics: The philosophical foundations of Hobbes's political thought', in Edmund Leites (ed.), *Conscience and Casuistry in Early Modern Europe* (Cambridge, 1988), p. 252.
12. Tuck has emphasized Hobbes's concern with overcoming scepticism and with developing a deductive and *a priori* science, in 'Grotius, Carneades and Hobbes', *Grotiana,* and 'Optics and sceptics'. Tuck claims that Hobbes maintains that people 'have direct acquaintance' with material objects, because perceptions '*are* material objects' (Tuck, *Philosophy and Government, 1572–1651,* p. 299). I disagree; acquaintance is an unmediated relation between two objects – a knower and the object known – it is not identity.
13. *Tractatus Opticus,* p. 147; quoted from Tuck, 'Optics and sceptics', p. 252; see also Tuck, *Philosophy and Government, 1572–1651,* p. 299. In the same passage, Hobbes misleadingly says that the hypothesis may be false. He later realized that he should have meant that the hypothesis from which a conclusion is inferred may not express the actual cause of the phenomena to be explained.
14. Tuck holds that Hobbes thought that people 'cannot be mistaken that our sensations are changing'; see 'Optics and sceptics', p. 254.
15. Hungerland and Vick think that the communicative use is the more basic one according to Hobbes; see 'Hobbes's theory of language, speech, and reasoning', in Thomas Hobbes, *Computatio Sive Logica* (New York, 1981), pp. 30–73. This view has been criticized effectively by Hugh Macdonald Ross, 'Hobbes's two theories of meaning', in *The Figural and the Literal*

(Manchester, 1987), pp. 31–57. There are also good but brief treatments of Hobbes's theory in J. W. N. Watkins, *Hobbes's System of Ideas,* 2nd edn (London, 1973) and Richard Peters, *Hobbes* (Harmondsworth, 1956).

16. Hobbes's definition of 'speech' is broader than the one that I have just given: 'Human vocal sounds, so connected as to be the signs of thoughts' (*DCo* 2.3).
17. The best treatment of Hobbes's use of the resolutive–compositive method is Watkins, *Hobbes's System of Ideas,* pp. 28–42; see also the commentary by Aloysius Martinich in Thomas Hobbes, *Computatio Sive Logica,* pp. 391–4, 414–17, and Hanson, 'The meaning of "Demonstration" in Hobbes's Science'.
18. For Harvey, see Watkins, *Hobbes's System of Ideas,* p. 42.
19. Saul Kripke, *Naming and Necessity* (Cambridge, MA, 1972), pp. 34–9, 122–3, 158–60.
20. M. M. Goldsmith, *Hobbes's Science of Politics* (New York, 1966), p. 178; cf. Frithiof Brandt, *Thomas Hobbes' Mechanical Conception of Nature* (Copenhagen, 1928), pp. 201–7; Shapin and Schaffer, *Leviathan and the Air-Pump,* pp. 80–1, 117–21, 123–4 and 380–1. For Hobbes, a serious problem with admitting the existence of vacuums is that, since he held that all motion takes place by contact, there seems to be no way of explaining motions through a vacuum.

5 HOBBES'S HISTORY OF ENGLAND, 1630–1660

1. J. G. A. Pocock, 'Time, history, and eschatology in the thought of Thomas Hobbes', in *Politics, Language, and Time* (New York, 1971), pp. 148–201; quotation from p. 201; see especially pp. 159–62. An interesting variation on Pocock's theme is Eldon Eisenach's *Two Worlds of Liberalism* (Chicago, 1981). His 'two worlds' are the secular world of liberty, in which a person is 'free to choose the best means of securing his preservation'and the second world of 'servitude', in which a person is 'bound to the commands of God, who intervenes at particular moments of history' (*Two Worlds,* p. 1).
2. Robert P. Kraynak, *History and Modernity in the Thought of Thomas Hobbes* (Ithaca, NY, 1990), pp. 17–18, 28. He bases his case on the Introduction to *De Cive* and chapter 46 of *Leviathan.* I do not

find support for it in either place; cf. *B*, p. 144. Hobbes refers to the 'three worlds' mentioned in the Bible: the old world (from Creation to the Flood), the present world (from the Flood to the day of judgement), and the world to come (from judgement day to eternity) (*L* 38.24, 44.32).

3. See Martinich, *Two Gods of Leviathan*, pp. 286–96.
4. Here is some speculation. History was not interesting as a process to most Christians because they did not believe it had any importance. With revelation completed with the death of the last Apostle, the next important event would be the second coming of Christ: everything in between was just one damned thing after another. Post-biblical history would have been significant if it involved long-term evolution. But it did not. No man knows the day or the hour of the second coming, because it comes like a thief in the night. Eschatological thinkers always find contemporary history interesting because they think it contains the immediate signs of the last times.
5. The interpretation that I am presenting is directly at odds with the influential view of Robert Kraynak, who thinks that Hobbes has an intrinsic interest in history because his first published work was a translation of Thucydides, and he wrote various histories of heresy and a history of the English Civil War (*History and Modernity in the Thought of Thomas Hobbes*, especially, pp. 7–31). My interpretation is consistent with these same facts about Hobbes.
6. See Miriam Reik, *The Golden Lands of Thomas Hobbes* (Detroit, 1977), p. 38.
7. Leo Strauss, *The Political Philosophy of Thomas Hobbes*, tr. Elsa Sinclair (Chicago, 1952). A good comparison of Thucydides and Hobbes is Laurie M. Johnson's *Thucydides, Hobbes, and the Interpretation of Realism* (De Kalb: Northern Illinois University Press, 1993); see also the review of it by David Grene in *Hobbes Studies*, new series, no. 19 (November, 1994), pp. 6–11.
8. During the Interregnum, some people had feared that the Episcopal Church would disappear completely. The episcopacy had been suspended in 1642. No new bishops were ordained between that time and 1660, and many of the pre-Civil War bishops died during that time.
9. On one interpretation, *Behemoth* is important because it shows that scholars have overemphasized the role of self-preservation in Hobbes's philosophy. Also, it allegedly shows that the ultimate foundation of his political authority is 'the opinion and

belief of the people', as Hobbes says there, and not physical force (Stephen Holmes, 'Introduction', *Behemoth or The Long Parliament* (Chicago, 1990), pp. x–xi). Holmes is referring to p. 16; but cf. pp. 29–30.

10. 'Revisionism' is the name given to the work of certain historians reacting against 'Whig' and Marxist interpretations. Roughly, revisionism denies that the Civil War was caused by long-term and structural problems in the constitution and maintains that the causes were in large part short-term and bound up with factionalism, regionalism and religion. For references, see R. C. Richardson, *The Debate on the English Revolution Revisited* (London, 1977).
11. Cf. Royce MacGillivray, *Restoration Historians and the English Civil War* (The Hague, 1974), p. 71. Hobbes is well-disposed towards James; see *B*, p. 34; *L* 19.23.
12. MacGillivray, *Restoration Historians,* p. 70, takes this to be a reference to Satan's temptation of Christ. I do not see that. I take Hobbes's allusion to be to the rock formation near Chatsworth, named the Devil's Arse.
13. Probably thinking of himself as a scientist, Hobbes is concerned with the causes of the war, not the events of the war themselves (*B*, p. 45).
14. To what extent does Hobbes blame Charles for his troubles? MacGillivray says not at all (*Restoration Historians,* p. 79). I think Hobbes does lay some blame on Charles, for example, for accepting the Petition of Right (*B*, p. 27).
15. MacGillivray, *Restoration Historians,* pp. 73–4, discusses the appropriateness of listing Roman Catholicism as a cause of the war.
16. The crucial passage is *B*, p. 72–3; see also MacGillivray, *Restoration Historians,* pp. 75–6.
17. Richard Tuck, *Philosophy and Government, 1572–1651* (Cambridge, 1993). There is an essay in the anonymously authored *Horae Subsecivae* (1620) that contains a commentary on the opening chapters of Tacitus' *Annals,* which some believe is by Hobbes. See, for example, Leo Strauss, *The Political Philosophy of Hobbes,* pp. xii–xiii, and Arlene Saxonhouse, 'Hobbes and the *Horae Subsecivae*', *Polity,* 13 (1980/81), 541ff. I am undecided.
18. Hobbes rightly thought that the excessive influence of London was a cause of the Civil War (*L* 29.21; *B*, p. 126).
19. C. B. Macpherson, *The Political Philosopy of Possessive Individualism* (Oxford, 1962); neo-Marxist interpretations can be found in

Frank Coleman, *Hobbes and America: Exploring the Constitutional Foundations* (Toronto, 1977), pp. 57–66, and Richard Ashcraft, 'Ideology and Class in Hobbes' Political Theory', *Political Theory*, 6 (1978), pp. 63–88. For a criticism of these views, see Keith Thomas, 'The social origins of Hobbes's political thought', in Keith Brown (ed.), *Hobbes Studies* (Oxford, 1965), pp. 185–236; and Kraynak, *History and Modernity in the Thought of Thomas Hobbes*, pp. 38–40.

20. *B*, pp. 36–7, 60, 84–5; *L* 18.19, 24.7, 29.10–1 1, 29.18.
21. Against various of these propositions, see *L* 18.4, 18.11, 18.12, 18.13, 18.14; see also *B*, p. 27, 101, 105–7.
22. Anthony Wood described Heath's book as 'being compiled from lying pamphlets, and all sorts of news-books' and as containing 'innumerable errors ... especially as to name and time'. Wood's quotation comes from MacGillivray, *Restoration Historians*, p. 12. See also Royce MacGillivray, 'Thomas Hobbes's history of the English Civil War: a study of *Behemoth*', *Journal of the History of Ideas*, 31 (1970), pp. 179–98.
23. The Scottish National Covenant is also attacked here. Hobbes is particularly offended that it was supposedly a 'covenant with God' (*B*, p. 28). On Hobbes's role in the Engagement Controversy, see Quentin Skinner, 'Conquest and consent: Thomas Hobbes and the Engagement Controversy', in *The Interregnum* (London, 1972), pp. 79–98; S. A. State, *Thomas Hobbes and the Debate over Natural Law and Religion* (New York, 1991), chapter 3; Richard Tuck, *Philosophy and Government, 1572–1651* (Cambridge, 1993), pp. 253–9.
24. On Hobbes's role in the Engagement Controversy, see Glenn Burgess, 'Contexts for the writing and publication of Hobbes's *Leviathan*', *History of Political Thought*, 11 (1990), pp. 675–702; Martinich, *The Two Gods of Leviathan*, pp. 354–61, and the literature cited in these two sources.

6 CONCLUSION

1. On this general issue, see W. V. Quine and J. S. Ullian, *The Web of Belief*, 2nd edn (New York, 1978), pp. 64–82.

Bibliographical Essay

This essay indicates only the main lines and most conspicuous research on Hobbes's thought. Many other valuable books and articles are mentioned in the notes to the chapters. The amount of excellent research that has been done on Hobbes, especially over the past three decades, is immense. The most extensive bibliography in English is William Sacksteder, *Hobbes Studies (1879–1979): A Bibliography* (Bowling Green, OH, 1982). Alfred Garcia's *Thomas Hobbes: Bibliographie Internationale de 1620–1986* (Caen, 1986) may be more comprehensive, but I have not seen a copy. The most important recent work is surveyed in Edwin Curley, 'Reflections on Hobbes: recent work on his moral and political philosophy', *Journal for Philosophical Research*, 15 (1989/90), pp. 169–250; and Perez Zagorin, 'Hobbes on our mind', *Journal of the History of Ideas*, 51 (1990), pp. 317–35. A more jaundiced survey is M. M. Goldsmith's 'The Hobbes industry', *Political Studies*, 39 (1991), pp. 135–47. E. G. Jacoby's review essay, 'Thomas Hobbes in Europe', *Journal of European Studies*, 4 (1974), pp. 57–65, is also helpful. For scholarly work on Hobbes published outside of the United States, the review of world scholarship on Hobbes published each year, beginning in 1988, in *Cahier* 2 of *Archives de Philosophie* is essential. It is under the direction of Y.-Ch. Zarka and J. Bernhardt. The journal *Hobbes Studies*, started in 1988 (Assen: Van Gorcum), and *International Hobbes Association Newsletter*, published from Colorado College, Colorado Springs, should also be noted.

Currently, the most complete sets of Hobbes's works are *The English Works of Thomas Hobbes of Malmesbury*, edited by Sir William Molesworth (London: John Bohn, 1839–45, 11 volumes), and *Thomae Hobbes Malmsburiensis Opera Philosophica Quae Latine Scripsit Omnia in Unum Corpus*, edited by William Molesworth (London: John Bohn, 1839–45, 5 volumes). This classic work is slowly being superseded by the Clarendon edition of the Works of Thomas

Hobbes. Volume 2, *De Cive*, edited by Howard Warrender, and Volumes 6 and 7, *The Correspondence of Thomas Hobbes*, edited by Noel Malcolm, are the only ones to have appeared. Three recent editions of Hobbes's *magnum opus, Leviathan*, count as important contributions to scholarship: Richard Tuck (ed.) *Leviathan* (Cambridge, 1991), Edwin Curley (ed.) *Leviathan* (Indianapolis, 1994), and Richard Flathman and David Johnston (eds), *Leviathan: A Norton Critical Edition* (New York, forthcoming in 1997). The French translation (Paris, 1971) is important because the translator François Tricaud pays close attention to the differences between the English and Latin versions.

Concerning Hobbes's life, the best place to begin is with John Aubrey's engaging biography in *Brief Lives* (Oxford, 1898, 2 volumes). There are several inexpensive editions of this work. It is then sensible to go to the various autobiographical writings in Volume 1 of Molesworth's *Opera Latina*. The verse autobiography, written in 1672, has been translated by J. E. Parsons, Jr. and Whitney Blair as 'The life of Thomas Hobbes', *Interpretation*, 10 (1981) pp. 1–7. (It contains some errors.) The prose life, dictated by Hobbes in 1676, has been translated by Mary Lyons and appears in Hobbes's *Human Nature and De Corpore Politico*, ed. J. C. A. Gaskin (Oxford, 1994). Written in the third person, *Mr. Hobbes Considered in his Loyalty, Religion, Reputation, and Manners. By Way of a Letter to Dr Wallis* (also known as *Considerations upon the Reputation, Loyalty, Manners, and Religion of Thomas Hobbes*) *EW* 4:409–40, is another enjoyable and informative source for Hobbes's own version of his life. There are several excellent recent accounts of all or part of Hobbes's life and thought. Johann P. Sommerville, *Thomas Hobbes: Political Ideas in Context* (London, 1992) emphasizes the political and religious aspects of Hobbes. Richard Tuck, *Hobbes* (Oxford, 1989) places him in an international context; he explains the influence of Grotius and Hobbes's interaction with Mersenne's circle. He sees Hobbes as responding to sixteenth-century scepticism by advocating materialistic science and an ethics built upon the idea of natural rights. *Thomas Hobbes: The Correspondence*, edited by Noel Malcolm (Oxford, 1994), has been described as 'stupendous' with no hyperbole. It contains all the known letters to or from Hobbes; the letters in French and Latin are presented both in their original form and in translation; and the book also contains notes and biographical sketches of most of the correspondents. Miriam Reik, *The Golden Lands of Thomas Hobbes* (Detroit, 1977) is sound and perceptive, but now showing its age because of the boom in Hobbes studies. The most complete biography available is Arnold Rogow, *Thomas Hobbes* (New York, 1986). It contains a great deal of information, but is mistaken about some details; and the author's speculations about Hobbes's psyche are often implausible. A classic account of Hobbes's intellectual life is George Croom Robertson's *Hobbes*, originally published in 1886; it has been republished (Bristol, 1993).

On the crucial stage of his intellectual development, essential reading is Richard Tuck, 'Hobbes and Descartes', in G. A. J. Rogers and Alan Ryan (eds) *Perspectives on Thomas Hobbes* (Oxford, 1988). Also in that volume is Noel Malcolm's essay 'Hobbes and the Royal Society', in which it is conjectured that an important reason why Hobbes was excluded from that body was that his thought was close to that of many of its members and the Society did not want to be tainted by his reputation. The other essays in the volume are also valuable for various aspects of Hobbes's doctrine and intellectual standing in Stuart England.

Several other collections of articles are excellent. Volume 6 of *Seventeenth Century British Philosophers*, edited by Vere Chappell (New York, 1992) is devoted to Hobbes. A classic is *Hobbes Studies*, edited by K. C. Brown (Oxford, 1965). Some of the articles in it are mentioned below. Another good collection is *Hobbes and Rousseau*, edited by Maurice Cranston and Richard Peters (New York, 1972). It contains Quentin Skinner's 'The context of Hobbes's theory of political obligation', a revised and abbreviated version of 'The ideological context of Hobbes's political thought', *Historical Journal*, 9 (1966), pp. 286–317. The most extensive collection of secondary material on Hobbes is collected in *Thomas Hobbes: Critical Assessments*, edited by Preston King (London, 1992, 4 volumes), which contains 122 items.

There are several excellent works that survey Hobbes's thought. Tom Sorrell, *Hobbes* (London, 1986) concentrates on Hobbes's epistemology, metaphysics and philosophy of science. Two older but still good treatments are J. W. N. Watkins, *Hobbes's System of Ideas*, 2nd edn (London, 1973) and Richard Peters, *Hobbes* (Harmondsworth, 1956). The use of more than 130 of Hobbes's concepts is surveyed in A. P. Martinich, *A Hobbes Dictionary* (Oxford, 1995).

Several historians have done excellent work in situating Hobbes within his historical context. The originator of this work is Quentin Skinner. In addition to the works by him mentioned above, one should note the following articles that concern aspects of Hobbes's political philosophy: 'Conquest and consent: Thomas Hobbes and the Engagement controversy', in G. E. Aylmer (ed.), *The Interregnum: The Quest for Settlement, 1646–1660* (London, 1972), pp. 79–98, and 'Thomas Hobbes on the proper signification of liberty', *Transactions of the Royal Historical Society,* 5th series, 40 (1990), pp. 121–51, and 'Thomas Hobbes: rhetoric and the construction of morality', *Proceedings of the British Academy,* 76 (1991), pp. 1–61. Richard Tuck places Hobbes in a broad tradition of modern moral and political theory in *Natural Rights Theories: Their Origin and Development* (Cambridge, 1979) and *Philosophy and Government, 1572–1651* (Cambridge, 1993).

Two books that were once very important for the interpretation of Hobbes are those by Leo Strauss and C. B. Macpherson. Strauss, in *The Political Philosophy of Hobbes* (Oxford, 1936), represents Hobbes as an arch-modernist and is good on Hobbes's early thought. Macpherson, in *The Political Theory of Possessive Individualism* (Oxford, 1962), represents Hobbes as defending bourgeois values, especially acquisitiveness. The definitive refutation of this thesis is Keith Thomas, 'The social origins of Hobbes's political thought', in *Hobbes Studies.* See also James Tully, 'After the Macpherson thesis', reprinted in *An Approach to Political Philosophy: Locke in Contexts* (Cambridge, 1993), pp. 71–95. Standing in the same class of powerful yet no longer persuasive interpretations is that of Michael Oakeshott in the Introduction of his edition of *Leviathan,* and in *Hobbes on Civil Association* (Oxford, 1975). He argues that Hobbes defined moral obligation as the command of the sovereign. Sheldon Wolin's, 'Hobbes: Political society as a system of rules', in *Politics and Vision* (Boston, 1960), is similarly a respected but dated treatment of Hobbes.

A great work on Hobbes's politics is David Gauthier, *The Logic of Leviathan* (Oxford, 1969). Gauthier distinguishes the form of Hobbes's theory, which he thinks is cogent, from its specific content, which he thinks is not. His book has spawned or influenced such rigorous treatments of Hobbes's political theory as Gregory Kavka, *Hobbesian Moral and Political Theory* (Princeton, 1986), and Jean Hampton, *Hobbes and the Social Contract Tradition* (Cambridge, 1986). David Gauthier, 'Hobbes's social contract', in *Perspectives on Thomas Hobbes* (Oxford, 1988), critically responds to Jean Hampton's book. The work of both Hampton and Kavka has been critiqued by Jody S. Kraus, in *The Limits of Hobbesian Contractarianism* (Cambridge,

1993). The title of David Johnston's *The Rhetoric of Leviathan* (Princeton, 1986) imitates and complements Gauthier's. It is one of the most important explanations of how Hobbes changed his approach in presenting his political philosophy. Richard Flathman, in *Thomas Hobbes: Skepticism, Individuality and Chastened Politics* (Newbury Park, CA, 1993) is quite different. He wants to relate Hobbes's thought to contemporary issues in political philosophy, and he argues that Hobbes intends the sovereign to have 'little effective authority and less power over its subjects'.

Other valuable works on Hobbes's political philosophy include M. M. Goldsmith, *Hobbes's Science of Politics* (New York, 1966) and F. S. McNeilly, *The Anatomy of Leviathan* (London, 1968), and Thomas Spragens, Jr., *The Politics of Motion* (Lexington, KT, 1973).

Two works that present Hobbes as a divine command theorist in morality are A. E. Taylor, 'The ethical doctrine of Hobbes', in *Hobbes Studies*, and Howard Warrender, *The Political Philosophy of Thomas Hobbes* (Oxford, 1957). The Taylor–Warrender thesis is that an action is moral if and only if God commands it. Taylor's article, which represents Hobbes as a Kantian, did not make an impact on Hobbesian scholarship until after Warrender's book appeared. There are discussions of Warrender's views in *Hobbes Studies*. An important criticism of Warrender is Quentin Skinner's 'Hobbes's *Leviathan*', *Historical Journal*, 7 (1964), pp. 321–33. A. P. Martinich's *The Two Gods of Leviathan* (Cambridge, 1992) revises the Taylor–Warrender thesis and accommodates what is correct about the views of their opponents.

Hobbes's religious beliefs are probably the most controversial aspect of his thought. The standard view has been that he was an atheist, or at best a deist. The best and most complete case for this position is Edwin Curley, '"I durst not write so boldly," or how to read Hobbes' theological–political treatise', in Daniela Bostrenghi (ed.), *Hobbes e Spinoza, Scienza e Politica* (Naples, 1992), pp. 497–593. Two important essays that advance the case that Hobbes was a genuinely religious thinker are Herbert Schneider's 'The piety of Hobbes' and Paul Johnson's 'Hobbes's Anglican doctrine of salvation', both published in Ralph Ross *et al.* (eds), *Thomas Hobbes in His Time* (Minneapolis, 1974). Martinich's book, *The Two Gods of Leviathan*, discusses a large part of this literature in the course of advancing the claim that two of Hobbes's projects in *Leviathan* were to show that Christianity is not politically destabilizing, and that Christian doctrine, reinterpreted, is compatible with modern science.

The classic treatment of Hobbes's scientific views is Frithiof Brandt, *Thomas Hobbes' Mechanical Conception of Nature* (Copenhagen, 1928). The chapter on Hobbes in Robert Kargon, *Atomism from Hariot to Newton* (Oxford, 1966) is very helpful. The most important recent discussion of Hobbes's philosophy of science is Steven Shapin and Simon Schaffer, *Leviathan and the Air-Pump* (Princeton, 1985).

Hobbes's mathematical ability has been denigrated ever since the 1650s. Very little objective investigation has been done on this matter. The best treatments of this issue are two articles by Douglas Jesseph, 'Hobbes on the methods of modern mathematics', *Revue d'Histoire des Sciences*, 46 (1993), pp. 153–93, and 'Of analytics and indivisibles', *Perspectives on Science*, 1 (1993), pp. 306–41.

For Hobbes's philosophy of language and logic, see the introduction by Isabel Hungerland and George Vick and the commentary by Aloysius Martinich in *Thomas Hobbes: Computatio Sive Logica* (New York, 1981). Their views are criticized by George Macdonald Ross, 'Hobbes's two theories of meaning', in Andrew E. Benjamin *et al.* (eds), *The Figural and the Literal* (Manchester, 1987), pp. 31–57. Hobbes's philosophy of language is also well-discussed in Willem De Jong, 'Did Hobbes have a semantic theory of truth?', *Journal of the History of Philosophy*, 28 (1990), pp. 63–88. Concerning the issue of how indebted Leibniz was to Hobbes, see L. Couturat, *La Logique de Leibniz* (Paris, 1901), pp. 457–72.

Hobbes's use of and views about rhetoric have been getting a lot of attention from scholars recently. The best place to begin this study is with David Johnston, *The Rhetoric of Leviathan* (Princeton, 1986). Other valuable works are as follows: *The Rhetorics of Thomas Hobbes and Bernard Lamy*, ed. John T. Harwood (Carbondale, IL, 1986); Quentin Skinner, 'Thomas Hobbes: rhetoric and the construction of reality', *Proceedings of the British Academy*, 76 (1990), pp. 1–61, '"*Scientia Civilis*" in classical rhetoric and in the early Hobbes', in Nicholas Phillipson and Quentin Skinner (eds), *Political Discourse in Early Modern England* (Cambridge, 1993), pp. 67–93; and *Reason and Rhetoric in the Philosophy of Hobbes* (Cambridge, 1996); Tom Sorell, 'Hobbes's unAristotelian political rhetoric', *Philosophy and Rhetoric*, 23 (1990), pp. 135–47; and Conal Condren, 'On the rhetorical foundations of *Leviathan*', *History of Political Thought*, 11 (1990), pp. 703–20, and the literature cited in it.

There is renewed interest in Hobbes's interpretation of the English Civil War. The best available account is Robert Kraynak's *History and Modernity in the Thought of Thomas Hobbes* (Ithaca, 1990), written from a Straussian perspective.

Index